WHOLE CHILD

PARENTING

INFANT
(Birth to 12 Months)

Concept by Claudia Sandor

WHOLE CHILD

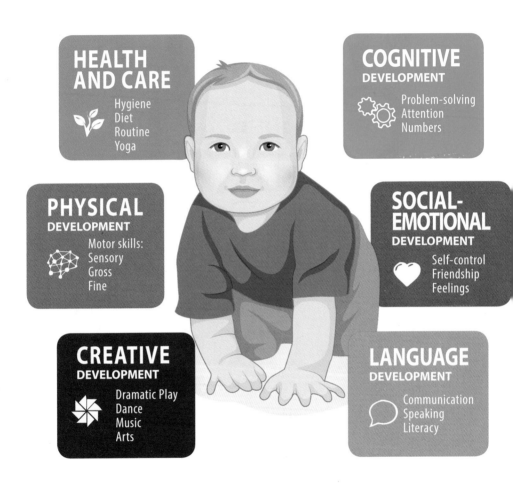

HEALTH AND CARE
Hygiene
Diet
Routine
Yoga

COGNITIVE
DEVELOPMENT
Problem-solving
Attention
Numbers

PHYSICAL
DEVELOPMENT
Motor skills:
Sensory
Gross
Fine

SOCIAL-EMOTIONAL
DEVELOPMENT
Self-control
Friendship
Feelings

CREATIVE
DEVELOPMENT
Dramatic Play
Dance
Music
Arts

LANGUAGE
DEVELOPMENT
Communication
Speaking
Literacy

WHOLE CHILD:
INFANT (Birth to 12 Months)
Six Areas of Development

WHOLE CHILD

whole \hōl\ **child** \chi-əld\ *compound noun*
1 : a child who is completely developed in all six areas

A **whole child**
grows up to reach
his or her full potential.

A **whole child** is a **well-rounded** person and lifelong learner.

A **whole child** is ready to face the world with **confidence.**

A **whole child** has **self-esteem, knowledge,** and **creativity.**

A **whole child** will live a **happy** and **fulfilling life.**

Being a successful parent starts with understanding your child.

The Whole Child Parenting Program covers every aspect of a child's cognitive, social-emotional, language, creative, physical, and health and care development.

By using clear examples, color-coded stages, simple and logical steps, age-appropriate materials and toys, developmentally appropriate activities and workbooks, and core parenting books, the Whole Child Program will change the way you think about learning.

Welcome to parenting for the new millenium!

Published by Whole Child Parenting, Inc.
Whole Child Parenting books, activity books, toys, and materials are
available at special discounts when purchased in bulk for premiums
and sales promotions as well as for fundraising or educational use.
For details, please contact us at:
sales@wholechild.co

Whole Child is a registered trademark of Whole Child, LLC
Library of Congress Control Number: 2016905513
ISBN 978-1-944930-04-2

Created by the Whole Child Education Team with:
Early Childhood Education Specialist, Erin Weekes
Book design by Willabel Tong
Art direction by Dan Marmorstein
Editorial direction by Editorial Services of Los Angeles

Visit us on the web at: www.wholechild.co
Email us at: publishing@wholechild.co

Printed in the United States of America.
1 3 5 7 9 10 8 6 4 2

Contents

Introduction:

**What Is Whole Child
Parenting?**   vi

Infant:

Milestones   2

Chapter 1:

Cognitive Development   4
Paying Attention   6
Mathematical Concepts   12
Cause and Effect   16
Problem Solving   18

Chapter 2:

**Social-Emotional
Development**   20
Social Development   24
Emotional Development   26

Chapter 3:

Language Development   32
Receptive Language   36
Nonverbal Language,   38
    Sign Language
Babbling   42
Cultivating Language   44

Chapter 4:

Creative Development   48
Music   52
Visual Arts   56
Dramatic Play   58

Chapter 5:

Physical Development   60
Perceptual Development   64
Gross Motor Skills   68
Fine Motor Skills   70

Chapter 6:

Health and Care   72
Hygiene, *Bathing, Ears, Eyes,*   74
    Nose, Tooth Care
Diet, *Hunger, Allergies*   80
Diaper Changing   86
Sleep, *Sleeping Safety,*   90
    How Much Sleep, Sleep Training
Mind and Body, *Yoga*   94

Reaching Milestones   96
Infant Environment   98
    Whole Child Room Elements

What Is Whole Child Parenting?

It Is Parenting from Head to Toe

Whole child parenting involves exposing your child to everything he needs to be happy, healthy, well adjusted, smart, and developing right on track. A whole child is a well-rounded person, someone whose innate talents have been developed in every major milestone category and who is ready to face the world with confidence. A whole child has the self-esteem and knowledge to develop his true potential.

Whole child parenting is you doing what you can, with our help, to get him there. The Whole Child Parenting Program is for busy people just like you. With interactive materials that support you at every step, using toys, workbooks, activities, videos, web support, and an app, the Whole Child Parenting Program takes into account the whole child and helps you, the parent or primary caregiver, do what is necessary and best for your child at every stage, every age from infancy to five years old. It helps you parent with a purpose, giving you practical advice and materials that explain the whys and how-tos and goals of each step you take to help your child grow.

Whole child parenting is a process that begins with you. It can be overwhelming to think about the responsibility you have to your infant in one of the most important years of his life.

This first year is a crucial year because development, in both the body and brain, is happening at a rapid pace. These first years will set the stage for how your child problem solves, communicates, socializes, and thinks for the rest of his life. That is not to say that you won't have amazing experiences with your child when he is an infant. You will have absolutely transformative experiences with your infant during these first twelve months. You will get to see life from the perspective of a new person! And **your presence and influence will always matter the most in this year and the next four years.** The world is constantly changing; will your child be ready for the global economy 18 years from now? Just by reading this book you are setting yourself along the right path for being the best parent you can be for your infant.

HOW TO GET ON THE RIGHT TRACK NOW

Whole Child Parenting: Infant has six chapters for the six areas of development seen in the column at right. **Each area of development is assigned its own color.**

Each of the six chapters begins with a chart and summary to introduce you to the concepts and terminology in the pages ahead. Within each chapter, **you will also get real-life activities and insights that paint a picture of how your child demonstrates these developmental concepts** in everyday life. In addition to examples, there are tips and advice

1 Cognitive
Development

2 Social-Emotional
Development

3 Language
Development

4 Creative
Development

5 Physical
Development

6 Health and Care

for parents and primary caregivers to use to support and guide you as you and your child encounter and master each of the upcoming milestones.

The Whole Child Parenting Program has developed five smart, modern, easy steps to help you raise a happy, thriving child.

> **The Whole Child Parenting Program involves:**
>
> 1. **Committing yourself**
> 2. **Educating yourself**
> 3. **Creating the right environment**
> 4. **Using the right materials**
> 5. **Staying on track**

That's it. Five steps to making your experience with your child the most rewarding and productive experience in your life.

STEP ONE: COMMITTING YOURSELF

Let's start with commitment. As a parent you have already taken the huge step of accepting responsibility for the little person in front of you— or soon to be in front of you. What is next required might not even be a step that needs articulating for you, but it bears repeating here: **You need to commit quality time to raising your whole child.**

There is no formula or script when it comes to being successful in parenting. Many parents look to doctors, textbooks, and experts for the secrets to parenting success. And while all of these are great sources, none address the whole child. And the whole child needs your attention. **Each child is different and has a different temperament, different interests, and a different personality.** As a parent, you are also different. Every parent has different values that come from being a part of different cultures, socioeconomic classes, education levels, religions, and family sizes. The best way to be successful in parenting is to be involved with your child. By being involved and communicating with your child, you are better able to support her and her needs.

Many wonder what the real measures and outcomes of good parenting are. It does not involve your child having a high IQ, being talented in sports, or making a lot of money. Good parenting results in raising a child who grows up to give back to society, is independent, has a good work ethic, gets along well with others, and understands her identity and self-worth.

When it comes to measuring your success as a parent, it is important to look at the quality of the relationship you have with your child and not how effectively you can control your child. Just because your child listens and follows the rules does not mean she understands or respects them; it just means she is obedient.

The quality of your relationship has to do with your involvement and communication with your child. Know what guidelines are appropriate to set for your child, and explain them in a way that shows why these rules are necessary and important. As a parent, you need to meet your child's needs and help her feel respected. This can be done by explaining the reasons behind rules and discussing your child's feelings and opinions.

When your child feels like she is a valued member of the family and the community, she will then develop the confidence needed to begin moving toward being independent and making her own decisions.

Parents who are uninvolved with their children tend to make their children feel ignored and unvalued. At the same time, parents who are overly controlling and establish strict rules over all avenues of their children's lives tend to make their children feel stressed and have low self-esteem. It is important to find the middle ground between controlling your child and overlooking your child.

Your child is born naturally impulsive, immature, and ambitious, and she looks to you for guidance and support. This is why it is important to **make sure you communicate clear guidelines and expectations** for your child to alleviate stress and misunderstandings.

THE FOUR STYLES OF PARENTING

Whole Child Parenting: Infant combines research, expert advice, and firsthand experience. In the past few decades, early childhood education has grown exponentially.

In the late 1950s, psychologist Erik Erikson organized development from birth to death into eight stages; according to Erikson, a person cannot successfully excel in the next stage of life without first completing the stage before.

Looking specifically at the first three stages, which cover ages birth to five, we see that a person's success lies first in his relationship with his parents. **Stage 1,** covering ages birth to two years old, focuses on a child's ability to develop **trust** with his parents. From there, children move on to **Stage 2** (for ages two to four years old), when the child is developing autonomy. **Autonomy** is your child's sense of self as an individual. Your child develops a sense of self by exploring the environment, learning about his own interests, and testing his limits. Moving forward to **Stage 3** (ages four to five years old), your child is **finding his purpose and place** within the family.

In the last 40 years, developmental psychologists have established **four styles of parenting.** The best parenting style is a combination of these four parenting styles—one in which you approach different situations with different solutions and always communicate with your child.

Authoritarian Parenting

The authoritarian parenting style can best be described as strict. Authoritarian parents tend to set rules that result in rewards or punishment if they are not followed. Rules are not explained and usually follow a reasoning of "because I said so." **These parents usually set high demands and expect obedience** but are not very responsive to their children. Children who grow up under the authoritarian parenting style tend to be obedient and usually well performing in school but socially exhibit signs of shame, low self-esteem, and lowered happiness levels.

Authoritative Parenting

The authoritative parenting style establishes rules and guidelines for children instead of just demands. Authoritative parents are more nurturing and forgiving, rather than simply punishing. They are responsive to their children and willing to listen and answer questions.

An important quality of authoritative parents is that they create clear standards for their children and adjust those standards based on their children's conduct.

Children who grow up under the authoritative parenting style tend to be capable and successful at learning new things. Socially and emotionally, they feel accepted and tend to be happy.

Permissive Parenting

The permissive parenting style is one that has few demands or guidelines. Parents tend to have low expectations for their children's maturity and abilities. **Permissive parents are more lenient with rules, preferring to avoid confrontation.**

This parenting style is usually nurturing and communicative but leaves children looking at their parent as more of a friend. Children who grow up under the permissive parenting style tend to often have poor self-regulation skills and may experience problems with authority and have trouble in school.

Uninvolved Parenting

The uninvolved parenting style is one with even fewer demands as well as little communication and responsiveness. Uninvolved parents fulfill their children's basic needs but tend to be detached and unavailable for their children in all other areas.

Children who grow up under the uninvolved parenting style tend to have low self-esteem, a hard time regulating their emotions, and a hard time making friends.

Your child's personality and temperament play a major role in how you choose your parenting style.

Research shows correlations between parenting styles and their impact on children. There is also evidence showing other factors, such as a child's personality and the outside environment, playing a role as well. Your larger environment— such as culture, religion, socio-economic class, and family style— can also affect how your child reacts to your parenting. School, friends, and personality play a significant role in how your child responds to your parenting style.

It is important to be consistent with your parenting style, especially when it comes to discipline and setting expectations for your child. Besides taking into account her environment, think about other people in your child's life, such as your spouse or partner or caregiver. Take time to talk to each other about parenting styles and how you will work together when raising your child. Talk about what you both value as important and how you were each raised; this is important for keeping your parenting style consistent.

At the end of the day, you need to remember to be present and realistic. **Be present both physically and mentally in order to be responsive to your child's needs.** Be realistic in your expectations and the guidelines you set for your child.

Committing quality time as a parent, whichever parenting style(s) you choose, is the single most important factor in your child's healthy development.

STEP TWO: EDUCATING YOURSELF

Addressing the whole child means knowing about the general developmental milestones your child will experience at each age. Milestones define peak stages of accomplishment when your child achieves the end of one stage before moving on to the next. **Milestones are exciting, because when a child reaches one you get to see how far she has come.** And you get to look forward to the next amazing stage your whole child will go through.

But how can you be aware of milestones without knowing the specific developmental categories the stages occur in? How can you have realistic expectations about what is age appropriate and what your whole child should or should not be doing? *Whole Child Parenting: Infant* **lays out six major developmental areas of your child's growth and follows them through this year of your child's development.**

Cognitive development

The first area of development is cognitive development. Cognitive development refers to the process of learning and the growth of intelligence and other mental capabilities, such as memory, reasoning, problem solving, and thinking. Memory and problem solving play a large role in your child's ability to engage in science, mathematical thinking, and logic.

Your involvement strengthens your child's cognitive abilities over these next years and plays a significant role in her school readiness and how she will learn and retain information later in life. At birth, your child's brain is only a quarter of the size of an adult brain; by age five, it has grown to be close to the same size and volume as yours.

Take advantage of these first five years to set the path and exercise the brain to its fullest potential. The Whole Child Parenting Program will very clearly define the stages of cognitive development and will help you be involved in your child's growth in this area.

Social-emotional development

Social-emotional skills reflect how effectively your child is able to interact in social settings. In order to interact well he must develop positive relationships. He must learn to recognize and regulate his emotions and reactions while communicating his feelings.

For young children, social-emotional skills provide a pivotal foundation upon which are built a range of other skills that are necessary in preschool as well as on play dates. Development in this category will help to determine how well your child succeeds with peer interaction throughout his life.

In order to interact well with others your child must develop positive relationships with others. He must also effectively coordinate his actions with communicating his feelings. As well, he must learn to recognize and regulate his emotions and reactions in many different social settings.

Your child needs to have good self-regulatory skills (i.e. the ability to calm himself down), keen emotional understanding (i.e. learning with help what made him feel the way he does), and growing communication skills such as naming how he feels and dealing with those feelings.

Language development

Language development is how your child communicates, from basic sounds and gestures to the use of pictures in books and words for speaking. As she ages your child will be communicating more than her emotions and needs. She will begin to tell stories, ask questions, and describe people and objects.

Your child will use memory to remember words and past events when telling stories. At an early age, your child's memory will also play a role in symbolic play when she uses props and objects as symbols to represent her ideas. These symbols will later translate to letter recognition and emerging literacy.

The Whole Child Parenting Program identifies how to use sign language to support early literacy skills, and we also include signs in supplemental and supportive materials in the program. Sign language for communication plays a role in your child's social-emotional development because it makes her better able to convey her emotions and needs when she is largely preverbal.

Creative development

Creative development involves how your child uses music, art, movement, and dramatic play to express himself and build imaginative thinking. When doing art, let your child make a mess and indulge in all the different textures and materials you provide. Make a paintbrush or other tools available to your child and then let him explore the paint with his hands. **Creative development plays a big role in your child's physical development as well.** Music and movement build your child's gross motor skills (big muscles) by allowing your child to test balance and large body movements. Visual art builds your child's fine motor skills (small muscles) by allowing him to explore materials such as scissors, paintbrushes, and crayons.

Creative development can be used as an avenue for social-emotional development. Through art and dramatic play, your child can express and act out feelings, model behavior, or work through emotions.

Through activities, examples, and tips, *Whole Child Parenting: Infant* shows how important creative development can be to your child's other areas of development as well.

Physical development

Physical development refers to your child's control over fine motor skills (small muscle movements of fingers, toes, and wrists) and gross motor skills (bigger movements that use the large muscles in the arms, legs, and torso). Between birth and five years old, your child's body and motor abilities make great strides.

Physical development has a lot to do with your child's self-esteem and sense of trust. Your child is more willing to test her physical skills of throwing, kicking, and balancing when she feels comfortable and confident within her environment.

Physical development is important because it plays a large role in children developing independence and self-help skills. Getting dressed, feeding themselves, and cleaning up are all skills that involve both fine and gross motor skills, which, when combined, develop sensory motor skills.

The Whole Child Parenting Program explains how your child's physical changes correlate with the development of motor abilities and overall physical growth and development.

Health and care

This section discusses safety, grooming, self-help, and the health of your child. As your child grows older, he will be more independent with his hygiene, from small achievements like brushing his own teeth to bigger accomplishments like potty training.

As he goes through each developmental stage, your child's body is changing and growing at a swift pace. He is growing taller, sprouting new teeth, and becoming more active, which will reflect in changes in his diet each year.

Whole child parenting also involves using yoga. Yoga is a great resource in which to engage your child from infancy through age four and beyond. Not only does it allow your child to explore his balance, but it also strengthens his social-emotional development by helping him find an avenue to calm himself. Yoga can also provide a bonding experience for parent and child.

Reaching Milestones

An important and exciting addition to our exploration of the six developmental categories is the Reaching Milestones section we provide at the end of the book. This assessment list will allow you to see everything your child should be doing and accomplishing developmentally around that age. Milestone assessments provide an exciting reflection of all that you are doing to support your whole child.

STEP THREE: CREATING THE RIGHT ENVIRONMENT

Now that you have committed your time and started educating yourself, it is time to follow through by setting up the right environment. Setting up an environment where your whole child will thrive plays a large role in all six areas of their development.

The importance of play

We are in a day and age in which there is an abundance of technology and information available to us. It is hard to remember a time when an answer to a question wasn't a mouse click away or we couldn't watch a video about how to fix something.

Technology has made our lives so much easier over the years, but that is not the case when it comes to our little ones. **Young children need to have the opportunity to make their own connections and discoveries within their environment.** Children between the ages of birth and three learn the most through play.

When setting up an environment that fosters **free play**, it is important to have child-sized furniture as well as incorporate baskets and trays for storing toys. Child-sized furniture and organizational materials such as bins and trays for different categories of toys help your child build independence and self-help skills. Being able to pick what he wants to play with from the shelf or bin will build upon your child's personal interests.

Just because your child is more in control of what activity and materials he is exploring in free play does not mean that you do not need to be involved in free play with your child. Setting up learning and play environments and making learning materials available is just part of encouraging free play. When watching your child explore materials in free play, it is important to interact with him.

The main aspect to remember about free play is that your child's interests guide it.

Structured play is also an important type of play and can help foster and build specific skills. Structured play differs from free play based on the fact that you are planning the activity and materials in which your child is engaging. You are leading the way with a specific activity that has a specific goal. Examples of structured activities can be doing a science experiment with your child or sorting different colored blocks. It is important to have both a combination of structured and free play activities available for your child.

Indoor environments

Incorporating child-sized furniture as well as baskets and trays for storing toys helps your child build independence and self-help skills.

Trays and baskets allow you to provide more manipulatives (age appropriate toys that foster growth) for your child and make it easier for your child to help care for and clean her environment. **When furniture and materials are at your child's eye level, she is able to have better control of her physical movements and be more aware of her environment.**

When setting up an environment that is beneficial for your child's language skills, it is important to have age-appropriate books available. Your child's interest in books both while reading with you as well as pretending to read on her own helps her relate words to pictures. Take your child's language learning to the next level and place labels like TABLE on your kitchen table. Your child will start making the connection between words and objects.

When doing art, let your child get messy and indulge in all the different textures and materials you provide. Investing in an easel, putting down a tarp, providing a smock, or buying washable paint can help you make your indoor environment fit for creative exploration. Having some paper and crayons out on a table that is child-sized makes expressing herself and her ideas easy. She can use the crayons to express herself creatively and create symbols that depict her feelings or needs.

Besides art materials, your child can express her thoughts and feelings through dramatic play by modeling roles and situations when dressing up or using props. Having a mirror in your child's room allows her to explore her self-concept skills. You will find your child making different faces in the mirror or watching herself stack blocks. Having a mirror that is at your child's eye level builds her self-concept by developing a better understanding of herself as an individual who has her own interests and ideas. Don't overwhelm your child with too many choices or structured activities, but instead follow your child's needs and interests to help encourage independence.

Your commitment to your child is very important when it comes to building attention span and memory skills. Having a rug or a chair that is child-sized will make your child more comfortable and thus want to spend longer on an activity. Your child's attention span is a cognitive skill, and it grows as your child grows older.

The Whole Child Parenting Program provides you with all the guidelines, furniture, educational books, activities, supplies, and toys for your whole child's stimulating environment.

Outdoor environments

Environments where your child can engage in free play allow him to develop self-identity and develop his own interests. He is able to learn more about himself by testing his cognitive and physical limits. There aren't always many opportunities for your child to fully engage in free play at home, which is why **outdoor environments provide beneficial play spaces for your child.**

By its nature, play is flexible, changeable, and multifaceted, so your child's play environment should reflect those criteria as well. Play is a core and vital component of how young children learn. Structured and unstructured play provide health benefits by allowing your child to be physically active as well as engaging in problem-solving and creative exploration.

Outdoor environments provide space and opportunities for structured activities that help children learn to communicate and work together, while unstructured activities in large, open areas help your child push limits and take risks.

Your child can make a mess, climb, shout, jump, and run as fast as he wants in open spaces. He can fully express himself and explore his body's movements. From this, your child will develop a sense of competence and confidence in his own physical abilities.

Large, open areas provide opportunities for your child to be creative and use his imagination. He can make connections and witness vivid colors, patterns, and textures in an outdoor environment.

Without material items, media, or structured rules, children can create their own games, engage in dramatic play, and entertain themselves through the use of their mighty imagination.

Nature provides an abundance of science and math opportunities that your child can explore and manipulate. Problem solving, learning cause and effect, and investigating use all of your child's senses. Your child will be exposed to nature and its elements and make connections by witnessing weather, ecology, growth, and natural life cycles. He can explore what happens when he throws a rock in a pond, adds water to dirt or sand, or watches snow melt.

It is not always easy to find a safe outdoor environment for your child. For families in the city, it may mean you need to travel a little farther, but the benefits are worth it. Outdoor environments can actually be considered cleaner than indoor environments, especially when it comes to germs.

By being in a large space with richly fresh air, germs and infectious agents are spread out. Indoor spaces tend to be more enclosed, which leaves bacteria to sit on surfaces and linger. Overall, the benefits of outdoor environments are enormous, and you need to take advantage of them.

How you set up your child's indoor and outdoor environments plays a large role in how he learns and develops. It is important to remember that you are a part of his environment and **in order for your child to thrive, he needs both a rich learning environment and your involvement.**

STEP FOUR: USING THE RIGHT MATERIALS

As parents, we frequently buy and invest in products and toys that are not age appropriate and serve no purpose developmentally, which is why the Whole Child Parenting Program has created developmentally appropriate tools and materials for the whole child that are both fun and educational.

When starting the Whole Child Parenting Program from infancy, you are able to build and adjust your child's environment and learning materials as she grows older. Many materials, such as toys and furniture, are able to grow with your child from infancy to kindergarten. Other materials, such as Whole Child Parenting activity books, toys, and parent resources, assist you with staying on track with your child's development while also helping you plan and measure your time and commitment to your child. The Whole Child Parenting Program is here to walk with you through these first five years.

A variety and quantity of materials are needed to accommodate young children's short attention spans. Children learn through concrete activities, and parents must be able to provide activities for both their physical, active needs and calm, quiet needs.

Having the right environment with both active and quiet play can help your child's social-emotional development by encouraging self-regulating skills. Having a quiet area to go to when your child feels overstimulated or needs a break is just as essential as having a safe area for her to be active and test her physical and creative limits.

A variety of materials is required

to stimulate the development of each age group. Some materials may fit into one or more categories; for example, an art activity can also serve as a fine motor exercise, and dramatic play can also act as a social-emotional tool.

It is important to remember that in order for your child to be able to explore and manipulate materials, she needs to have the materials made easily available to her at all times of the day. Setting up the right environment and investing in furniture that is both safe and easily accessible will play an important role in supporting your child's development.

STEP FIVE: STAYING ON TRACK

Once you have set up your environment, the Whole Child Parenting Program makes staying on track easier by providing you with activity books, toys, and learning materials. Consistency and routine play a big role in your whole child's development, so it is up to you to follow through and use these materials with your child.

Five years may seem far away, but time always has a way of sneaking up on us. In the blink of an eye, your child will be five years old and boarding the bus for school. This is a big milestone in your child's life, but you will be confident your child is ready for school because the Whole Child Parenting Program has helped you stay on track with your child's development. Your child is leaving for school a confident, happy, healthy learner.

In the end, all we want for our children is for them to be happy and confident because happiness and confidence set your child on the road to success. The Whole Child Parenting Program is here to get you to that point so you can take a deep breath and know your child is ready to face the world.

Through our *Whole Child Parenting: Infant* book, educational materials, and workbooks, tips, and activities, apps, videos, and web support, you will have the tools to build a relationship with your child that allows him to confidently express himself through his creative and social-emotional skills, which in turn help him build his cognitive, language, and physical skills. You want your child to be healthy, happy, and complete, developing at or ahead of the curve. The Whole Child Parenting Program was developed for you, the committed and caring parent.

infant >
(Birth to 12 Months)

Milestones for an Infant

 **COGNITIVE** 1

- Develops vision
- Uses vision to focus on objects
- Explores with cause and effect
- Begins thinking and problem solving

 **SOCIAL-EMOTIONAL** 2

- Learns to develop trust and security
- Expresses and understands emotions

 LANGUAGE 3

- Develops an understanding of verbal communication
- Communicates wants and needs through smiles and cries
- Experiments with sounds

 CREATIVE 4

- Creates music through playing with sound
- Develops spatial intelligence through art experiences
- Starts building the foundations for dramatic play

 PHYSICAL 5

- Uses senses to control large and small motor movements
- Learns to roll over, sit up, crawl, stand, and walk
- Uses touching and grasping for learning

 HEALTH AND CARE 6

- Uses self-soothing skills
- Starts solids at four to six months
- Begins to boost physical strength and skills

infant
(Birth to 12 Months)

Your baby has arrived! You've made it through the excitement of labor and delivery, and now you're ready to head home and begin life with your baby. This is a time to develop the bonds that will last a lifetime, providing your child a vital foundation influenced by the caring and nurturing relationship you build. This foundation will help your child develop self-esteem and the ability to relate positively with others.

1. Cognitive Development

> **Cognitive development refers to the way your infant uses his brain to process information.**

Your baby processes information through problem-solving events, using his memory, and thinking, and reasoning through everyday experiences.

In your baby's brain, there are a hundred billion neurons, also known as brain cells. All of these brain cells connect together as your baby grows; this is what makes your baby smarter. Connections are formed by all of the wonderful experiences you provide for your baby to learn.

Your baby is born with a strong desire to soak up information and learn through the things he sees, hears, smells, tastes, and touches. He then stores the information, sorts it out, and uses it now and in the future.

In order for all this information to soak in, there are two very important things your baby must have; these two things stimulate learning so that connections can be made. These two important things are *relationships* and *emotional support*. Relationships provide your baby with a secure emotional base from which he can learn and explore. A secure emotional base enables your baby to feel safe, feel confident, engage with others, and seek support from you when needed as he takes in information.

The following chart provides you with an image that walks you through your child's stages of intellectual development.

Understanding these areas of cognitive development will help you learn how your child thinks, how to support learning, and how to teach new skills.

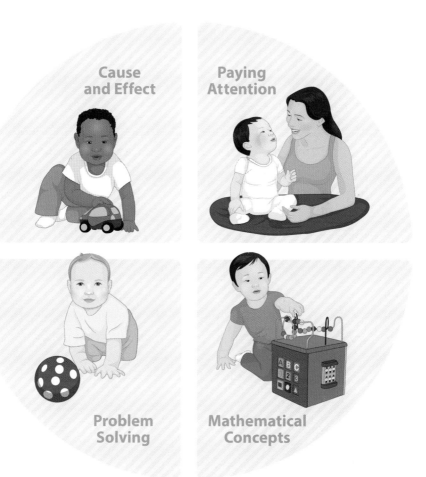

Cause and Effect

Paying Attention

Problem Solving

Mathematical Concepts

Whole Child: infant
Cognitive
Development Components

Paying Attention >
Vision

Visual development in your baby sets the stage for cognitive development as she uses her sense of sight.

What else can your baby see?

* Your baby can see 8 to 15 inches in front of her.

* At one month, she will pay attention to the hairline of a parent.

* At two months, your baby will give more attention to the eyes on a face.

* At three months, your baby will focus on your facial expressions.

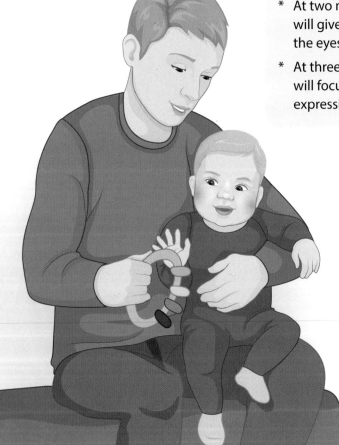

Visual Development

Your baby must have the ability to develop sight and focus her attention on you, other people, and objects. This occurs as your baby starts glancing around, looking at the faces of her parents, and seeing smiling responses. As her vision becomes more refined, your baby will use her eyes to focus on colors and respond to sounds by looking toward the sound.

Let's take a moment to talk about your baby's sense of sight during this age. Despite your baby's limited visual development, the moment you and your baby make eye contact for the first time she is developing her ability to focus her attention on you.

The more your baby makes eye contact during the first month after birth the more she will develop a preference for looking at your face.

It is very important for primary caregivers to keep their facial appearance unchanged after the baby is born. Limit your use of scarves and caps; don't get a new hair color or a drastic haircut after your baby is born; she does not care if your hair is done. She just wants to see your face and feel your touch; this is what makes her feel safe and comfortable.

In addition to having a preference for looking at their primary caregivers' faces, your baby is only able to see in black and white and shades of gray upon birth because the nerve cells in the back of her eyeballs are sensitive to light, but her vision is not fully developed.

Your baby will develop her ability to see color a few days after birth. At one week old, your baby will see red, orange, yellow, and green. These colors are more stimulating for your baby, so use them instead of pastels in your baby's room for mobiles, decorations, and curtains.

By six months, your baby's visual ability has grown tremendously; she is now able to see things more clearly and quickly. Your baby's vision is now 20/25, and she can see all the colors of the rainbow (red, yellow, orange, purple, blue, and green).

At six months of age your baby should have her first eye exam. Your pediatrician will check for nearsightedness (your baby can see closer objects) and farsightedness (closer objects are blurry); both are related to how light is focused as it enters your baby's eyes.

Your physician will also check for astigmatism, which occurs when your baby's eye is shaped more like an American football. If astigmatism is present, the light that is projected onto the retina is distorted, causing your baby to see a blurred or distorted image.

Support your baby's visual development by positioning yourself in her line of sight. Once she focuses, move your face so she follows you with her eyes. This will develop visual tracking skills.

During the period of 7 to 12 months of age, your baby is developing her ability to coordinate her vision with her attention span and to focus for two to three seconds on patterned objects of stripes and checks as opposed to solid-colored objects.

ACTIVITY

 Dad is having some alone time with seven-month-old Ethan. He lays Ethan on his cloth ring on the floor, and then Dad takes his keys out of his pocket and slowly jingles them in front of Ethan's face. Ethan looks up at Dad and stares at the keys intently. Dad jingles and moves the keys from the left side to the right side and watches Ethan follow the keys with his eyes. Many times Ethan reaches up and attempts to grab the keys. As Dad sees this he lowers the keys a little bit so Ethan can touch them. Dad repeats this activity several times until Ethan is ready to move on to another activity.

INSIGHT

 Because the keys are shiny and jingle, they reflect the light and catch Ethan's attention. The light shining on the keys is letting Ethan's eyes tell his brain that there is something interesting about these keys. This is what leads Ethan to explore the keys by reaching and touching them. Ethan is demonstrating his attention and hand-eye coordination skills. In the blink of an eye, he can reach out and touch an object, something that previously only happened by chance.

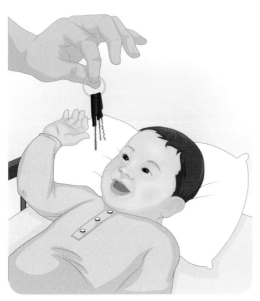

Visual development is important for your baby because to grow he needs to use the visual information his eyes send to his brain to understand the world around him and interact with it appropriately. You play an important role in helping your baby's eyes develop properly. To support your baby's visual skills, try the following activity.

ACTIVITY

Make a tissue paper sun catcher. For the sun catcher, cut colored tissue paper into various sizes, lay a 4" x 5" sheet of waxed paper on a table, and brush the paper with white glue diluted with a few drops of water. Then place the tissue paper on top of the glue and let it dry (approximately 20 minutes). Make a hole at the top for yarn.

Using your sun catcher, hold it up in front of your baby's face. Give your baby a moment to see the sun catcher, then move it slowly from left to right, right to left, and up and down.

INSIGHT

When you see that your baby has stopped looking at it, stop and give him a moment to focus again on the object and repeat the process. Through this simple activity, you are giving your baby time to see color changes; develop tracking skills, attention, and focus; and use visual information.

Visual Attention

Visual attention is defined as your baby's ability to focus or concentrate on an object. This can only occur once your baby's vision has matured.

There is a link between cognitive development and visual attention with your baby. The duration of time your baby can focus on an object is related to an increase in her cognitive function.

As attention span increases with your baby, she also develops higher-order attention abilities or sustained attention that will be used throughout childhood and well into adolescence.

Let's visualize the timeline by which your infant develops focused attention. From birth to three months, your baby goes from sleeping all the time to developing periods of alertness and watching things in her environment (e.g. primary caregiver's hairline).

During the three- to four-month period, your baby combines alertness with her ability to visualize where objects are in her environment (e.g. colored objects with patterns). She can see if the object is in front of her or to the side or when the parent moves the object up or down, thus developing her peripheral vision (objects seen at the side edges of sight) and her ability to track where the object is.

Birth to 3 months	3 to 4 months	5-½ to 12 months
Your baby goes from sleeping all the time to developing periods of alertness and watching things in her environment.	Your baby combines alertness with her ability to visualize where objects are in her environment.	As you provide more interesting objects for your baby to see, she will develop her attention skills.

As you provide more interesting objects for your baby to see during the 5½ to 12-month period, she will develop her attention skills. More interesting objects include toys that are full of bright, primary colors, make noises (squeaking toys and electronic toys), and can be manipulated in a variety of ways (e.g. a mobile attached to the bar of a car seat).

Developing visual attention in your infant is important for three reasons:

1. It enables your baby to develop social skills because she must rely on you to provide visual stimulation and interaction opportunities.

2. Because your baby is restricted by her inability to move around on her own in those pre-crawling months, she needs toys on which she can focus in order to explore her environment and gain knowledge about the world around her.

3. Your baby's ability to visually focus her attention on her mother's or father's face leads to establishing a bond with her parents or other primary caregivers.

We have talked about why visual attention is important for your infant; we must also note an important skill developing in your three to nine month old. This is attention control and refers to your baby's ability to choose what she pays attention to and what she ignores. This is what enables your infant to actively explore her environment despite what is going on around her.

As your baby matures, her ability to exercise attention control will continue to increase. This will play a critical role in your baby's cognitive and social-emotional development later in life. For instance, if your baby never forms quality emotional attachments with you as the parent or primary caregiver, she will experience periods of anxiety and uncertainty. This will lead to decreased attention control, thus preventing the development of your child's ability to stay on task, and affecting her ability to engage in social settings.

Mathematical Concepts >

Supporting Early Math Skills

Mathematical concepts are important components of rational and logical thinking.

As your infant interacts with his environment and with people in his world, he will use math concepts to make sense of the world in which he lives.

Infants develop math skills in the first year of life and are natural mathematicians. Your baby was born with an understanding of math concepts that involve quantities (e.g. when he cries because he wants more of his bottle or food).

Patterns provide another math concept for infants. Your infant's ability to experience patterns and routines enables him to become a logical thinker and to understand how his environment works in a predictable way. For instance, as you care for your baby, he begins to recognize and anticipate a pattern of sequential activities that demonstrate how you will care for him on a daily basis.

You can play games with your infant, such as Pat-a-Cake or Peek-a-Boo to allow your baby to experience sequences and patterns.

As your infant recognizes patterns, he will also begin to understand **sequencing**. Sequencing is a particular order in which related events or things follow each other. Recognizing sequences helps your infant develop a sense of order, logic, and reasoning. Your baby sees the sequences of activities within his day and is able to predict what may happen next.

By age one, your child will become more involved with activities that require sequencing, such as waking up, eating breakfast, washing up, and brushing teeth. This is a sequence of events for your child.

Becoming aware of similarities and differences is awareness of **sorting** and **classifying**, which are mathematical concepts used in learning. As your infant approaches 11 months, he will learn the concepts of *more* and *enough*, which are two of the first number concepts that children develop.

ACTIVITY

It is lunchtime, and Dad makes nine-month-old Jacob a lunch of carrots and soup. After Jacob finishes the tomato soup, Dad gives Jacob a carrot. Jacob eats the first carrot, but as Dad gives Jacob another one, he hears Jacob say "No, no" and shake his head.

INSIGHT

Jacob says "No, no" when he is satisfied with the amount of carrots he is given. Jacob demonstrates an understanding for *enough*, which is an early math concept.

ACTIVITY

 Gently bouncing your infant on your lap as the other parent claps to the beat will demonstrate that beats are related to number concepts such as counting and one-to-one correspondence (e.g. one bounce for one beat).

INSIGHT

Math concepts can be introduced very early on. And music provides an enjoyable, entertaining way to learn, explore, and develop cognitive skills. It has been demonstrated that the parts of the brain that become active when music is played are the same ones that become active when math is practiced.

There are lots of opportunities during your baby's day to discover math concepts through play and to hear new math words.

At around a year of age, your infant will try to fit objects into various sizes of containers, which is the beginning of learning geometry (shapes and space). As your child approaches age two, he will learn how to do simple puzzles.

Even though your baby was born with a basic mathematical understanding, parents and other adults that interact with your infant have a very important role to play.

Your infant will develop and refine math concepts and skills through the routines, experiences, and interactions you have with him each day. By being aware of these early mathematical concepts, you can be more intentional in how you support your baby's math learning as well as school readiness as time goes on.

Math is everywhere; it is a way of thinking and problem solving. You use it more with your infant than you may realize. Think about the last time you played This Little Piggy with your infant's fingers or toes. As you take one finger or toe at a time to do the rhyme, you are showing your infant the math concept of sequential order.

Support your baby's development of mathematical concepts by using math talk, such as "You have two eyes and so does your bear. Let's count: one, two." You can also say, "You have two bottles. Let's start with the one that has more formula (or breast milk)."

Think about how many ways you are using math in your interactions with your baby. Remember, the key is to intentionally introduce math concepts every day with your baby.

The more you engage your infant in math play and math talk, the better chance he will have to develop the early math foundations necessary for learning math well into adulthood.

Activities to support mathematical development:

1 to 4 months:
Read board books that incorporate math concepts.

4 to 8 months:
Find materials with different textures (smooth satin, bumpy washcloths, soft cotton). Rub them over your baby's arms, legs, and bottoms of his feet and talk about how they feel. Fill empty water bottles with baby powder, cotton balls, or paper clips. Seal the top and let your infant explore them.

8 to 12 months:
Tie colored scarves together and put them in a paper towel tube with a little bit sticking out. Let your baby pull the scarves through the tube. Lay out boxes for your baby to crawl through, and talk about what your baby is doing as he crawls.

Cause and Effect >
Actions Bring Responses

Cause and effect refers to
the relationship between an
action and its outcome.

Understanding cause and effect
starts with your baby interacting with
her environment and then learning
an action that will lead to an effect.

This is the beginning of her ability
to understand cause and effect. For
instance, each time your baby cries,
she begins to learn that you will pick
her up or use an object such as a
rattle to distract her.

If your baby were to also shake the
rattle, she would hear a sound; when
she drops the rattle on the floor, she
sees it disappear. Through play, your
baby is learning that she can cause
things to happen or change.

ACTIVITY

 Mom shakes a rattle in front of Chelsea and says, "See the rattle?" As Chelsea is sitting in her high chair she reaches for the rattle and grabs hold of it with a fist grip.

Chelsea then drops the rattle. Mom picks up the rattle and hands it back to Chelsea. As soon as Chelsea gets ahold of the rattle again, she drops it on the left side of the high chair. Chelsea's eyes are fixed to the floor as she drops the rattle.

Mom picks up the rattle again, saying "Oops! The rattle fell on the floor!" Mom hands the rattle back to Chelsea. Chelsea takes the rattle in her hand, looks at it, and then drops it on the right side of the high chair, keeping her eyes fixed on the rattle that has fallen to the floor.

INSIGHT

Chelsea is experimenting with what happens when she drops the rattle. She watches it fall to the ground on both sides of her high chair. She will continue to drop the rattle (cause) and see it fall to the ground (effect). This activity will test your patience; however, it is an important way for your baby to learn about cause and effect and her ability to influence her environment.

As your baby grows older, her memory is developing. You'll start to see her absorbing information and applying it to her day-to-day activities.

During this period, one of the most important concepts she is using in cause-and-effect situations is her memory. We previously discussed your baby reaching toward an object that makes noise and dropping it on the floor. As your baby understands that she can cause these interesting reactions, she will continue to experiment with other ways to make things happen.

Think about each time you sing a particular song as you feed your baby; she will begin to anticipate the song and the feeding each time you begin the activity. The same goes for when your baby interacts with another family member and learns that by laughing she makes that person smile; she will then laugh again to get the same effect. These experiences with your infant will increase social skills and set the stage for symbolic and language learning.

Problem Solving >
Thinking

Your baby is learning how to get what she wants, when she wants it; this is also called thinking and problem solving.

During the first year of your baby's life, she is making great strides in her ability to think, solve problems, and communicate with you. These are critical cognitive skills.

For instance, your baby thinks to herself, *I want that rattle!* Your baby solves the problem by deciding to roll over and reach for or crawl to the rattle. Maybe your baby is thinking, *I am hungry!* She solves the problem by communicating through cries, grunts, or pointing until you feed her.

Once you are sure your infant's basic needs have been met and she is not in any danger, it is important to give your baby time to work on problem-solving skills.

Think about times you have just put your baby in the crib, and she immediately begins to cry as you turn to leave the room. Even though you may want to pick her up again and rock her longer, this is a great opportunity to let your infant work on her problem-solving skills, namely the skill of being able to self-soothe and see what she can do to make herself comfortable enough to go to sleep. It is certainly hard to listen to the cries, especially when it is your first baby, but as your baby matures, she will need to be able to put herself to sleep.

It is also very important to support problem-solving skills when your baby is learning to feed herself a bottle or use a spoon. Infants as young as six months have been known to feed themselves; they won't get all the food on the spoon or even in their mouths, but they are developing self-help skills and problem-solving skills. They are also developing their wrist muscles and fine motor skills (small muscle skills).

When you support problem-solving skills with your infant, you are supporting her brain development and giving her the power to think and constantly learn about the world around her.

Support your baby's problem-solving skills by responding to her efforts to communicate. Use words to describe what she is experiencing: "I see you looking at the toy on the floor. Let me get that for you." Talking to your child and explaining what you are doing when you do it also increases language development.

Your infant's problem-solving development:

0 to 2 months—Your infant is born with built-in problem-solving tools called *reflexes* (rooting and sucking for food).

2 to 4 months—Your infant is more alert; she explores; hand-eye coordination begins to develop and bringing toys to mouth leads to problem solving.

8 months—Your infant plays with toys to produce responses to actions by grasping, shaking, and banging.

12 months—Your baby uses more purposeful levels of problem solving and is no longer limited to what is immediately in front of her. She can now push a toy aside to choose another one.

Remember, the Whole Child Parenting Program
offers appropriate developmental products and monthly activity books that walk you through supporting your child's skills. Using these in conjunction with the recommended age-appropriate room materials ensures faster development.

2. Social-Emotional Development

> **Social-emotional development begins in infancy and involves your baby bonding with you and developing a trusting, secure, and safe relationship with you.**

When your baby is soothed by a parent's voice it sets her on the right path emotionally. Reading your baby's cues and attending to her needs from the day she is born starts off her social-emotional development on the right track. When your baby is born, she has no idea who you are; she doesn't know what role you will play in her life. Fear overcomes her initially; she cries because she has been taken out of her warm, safe environment (the womb).

For this reason, it is important to hold your baby as soon as you can when she is born. Lock eyes with her, hold her, and speak softly to give comfort, letting your baby know that you are here and she is safe.

WHOLE CHILD: INFANT
Social-Emotional
Development Components

Babies are not born with social skills; they develop as the baby grows. Your role as the parent or primary caregiver is to teach and encourage these abilities. By doing so, you give your baby a sense of who she is in the world. By helping her learn who she is, you affect how she will learn and how she will develop relationships with others; you also start her on the path to having positive self-esteem.

1. Social Development

Social development is the process through which your baby learns how to interact and express herself with others. This process is taught by you. The way you react to your baby's needs and cues helps build social connections.

2. Emotional Development

Emotional development is the process in which your baby learns to recognize and express her feelings and to establish a personal identity independent from you. Parents and primary caregivers play a big role in their baby's emotional development when they help babies learn to express their feelings.

Parents, family, and caregivers interacting with the baby from the very start helps the child form bonds that later will encourage her to build other satisfying relationships.

Remember, the Whole Child Parenting Program offers appropriate developmental products and monthly activity books that walk you through supporting your child's skills. Using these in conjunction with the recommended age-appropriate room materials ensures faster development.

Social Development >
Forming Relationships

Social development reflects your baby's growing trust in you and how secure she will feel in the world.

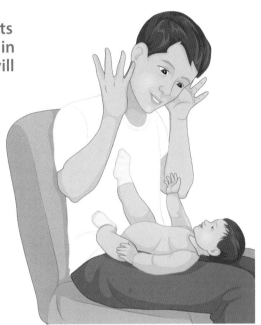

More awareness is being placed on the foundation of social development during the first three years of life. This foundation will be reflected in your child's ability to be successful in relationships, with the additional belief in her ability to achieve any goal she puts her mind to.

ACTIVITY

Four-month-old Holly is sitting with Dad in the chair. Dad holds his hands over his face and then swings his hands out and says, "Peek-a-boo, Holly! I see you!" Each time Dad shows his face, Holly laughs. When Dad tries to stop the game Holly kicks her arms and legs to let Dad know she wants to keep playing the game. Dad decides to continue to play the game until Holly loses focus and wants to move on to something else.

INSIGHT

Holly is discovering that relationships with people in her environment are fun and satisfying. Through this experience Holly demonstrates her ability to follow Dad in whatever he is doing. As well, Holly is letting Dad know that wherever Dad may go, she wants to interact and be with him.

When your baby is secure in her relationship with you, she then knows that no matter what happens you will be there emotionally, and you will show her how to form strong, positive relationships with others.

During the first three years of life your baby is working hard to develop trust and relationship skills. Your baby learns social skills first by using her eyes, next by turning her head to see you, and then by observing what you are doing around her. She finally ends with adding her body to the experience. This is why it is so important for your baby to stare into your eyes and fall in love with you shortly after birth. Your baby is learning who she is by how she is treated.

Parents play a big role in their babies' social development by sending messages like "I love you. You're such a smart baby. I love being with you. You are such a funny baby." Verbal messages like these will help form your baby's self-esteem.

Because the bond with you is becoming so strong there will be times during your baby's social development when she will have stranger and separation anxiety, which is apparent when a fear of unfamiliar people occurs and is expressed by your baby crying.

Separation anxiety is a normal part of social development; however, it does require your emotional support to let your infant know that the social encounter is a safe one, and she does not need to fear. This support can be given through touch; cuddles; a calm, soothing voice; and just taking the time to play an interactive game. For example, in the afternoons when your baby gets grumpy and it's not time for a nap, nothing works better than dancing with her. Put on some music and hold her in your arms. A good distraction is silly exaggerated movements like jazz hands (fingers splayed, wrists twisting), which are funny to your baby.

Parents have relationships with extended family and friends on a routine basis. Talk with these people when appropriate about your baby's likes and dislikes, what calms her and what upsets her. Working with extended family and others who may spend time with your baby helps to ensure that she will feel safe and secure with all relationships.

Social development is also learned through play experiences you provide for your baby. Your baby will learn about the world around her through play, and play builds all areas of her development.

Emotional Development >
Feelings

Emotional
development is how
your baby begins to
develop the capability
to experience, express,
and understand
emotions.

ACTIVITY

Chad is in his crib sleeping when all of a sudden he breaks out in a very loud cry. Mom hears his cry on the baby monitor and goes into the nursery to see what is wrong. Mom says, "Chad, what's wrong, buddy? You were sleeping so well." Mom picks up Chad out of his crib, holding him close to her chest. Mom then discovers that he is wet straight through his diaper and his onesie.

INSIGHT

Crying is how Chad is expressing feelings, and he should be allowed to do so. Rather than using distractions to try to stop your baby from crying, try to figure out why the crying is occurring so that you are able to help. Here, Chad is signaling his discomfort to Mom through his cry, letting her know that something needs to be addressed so he can get back to enjoying his sleep.

Babies learn emotions through interaction with parents and caregivers. **Parents have a significant influence on how their children turn out, including their personalities, emotional development, and behavioral habits.** For instance, one important emotional reaction is crying, which is part of a baby's emotional development.

Before your baby is four months old, you must build trust and a sense of security by attending to his basic needs, which are feeding, comforting, and cleaning.

It is important for you to know the different types of cries your baby might have so that you can determine what type of comfort he needs. Understanding your baby's cry also includes understanding his temperament.

Your crying baby can be consoled with motion, cuddling, singing, massage, or a toy. But this will only last so long; at some point, these techniques will have to be added to the child's taking a more active role in feeling better. **Some babies self-soothe by sucking on a thumb or a pacifier, gazing at objects, or using other sensory experiences to calm down.** Your infant will learn to self-soothe if you give him a

An emotionally available parent will have the following characteristics:

Sensitive—is conscious of the infant's cues, understands those cues, and provides support;

Structured—creates a sleep environment that is positive, quiet, and soothing on a consistent basis;

Nonintrusive—recognizes that a baby needs quality sleep and does not create or allow distractions;

Nonhostile—does not display frustration or anger when engaged in routines with the baby such as changing or going to sleep.

chance. The most important concept to understand is you must listen to your baby and learn to understand his cries to determine the root cause first, then move on to one of the techniques mentioned.

A crying baby can be emotionally draining for a parent. **It is important to understand that your baby is influenced by your emotions, tone and volume of voice, gestures, and facial expressions.** Your baby needs to feel affection and caring despite how you are feeling emotionally or physically.

Being physically present is not enough. When parents are just nearby and not emotionally invested in their babies or are not responsive, they are raising children who will be distressed and less engaged with their play or activities or other people. It is important for the overall development of your infant to be present enough to support him emotionally; this support will foster confidence and growth in all aspects of the whole child.

A critical time to be emotionally available is at bedtime. **Babies from one to 24 months sleep better when parents are emotionally available at bedtime.** When you are there to address needs it is easier for your baby to fall asleep and sleep through the night.

An emotionally available parent makes the baby feel safe.

As a parent, you need to adapt to your baby's temperament, because it is his unique emotional makeup. Take time to see what temperament your infant is developing; it will enable you to adapt to your baby's emotional makeup and support his needs.

A key aspect of emotional development in babies is learning how to regulate emotion. Your baby was born with little self-control, so he acts and reacts without the ability to stop himself.

When you have an understanding of the kind of temperament your baby has, you can provide better guidance to help him begin to manage his emotions. Furthermore, how you address the emotions of your infant and respond to him affects how expressive your baby will feel he can be later in life. The temperaments of parents and caregivers and the emotional climate of the home will influence emotional development. Therefore, make sure you have all the support you need to be emotionally present for the needs of your little one.

Let's explore some temperament traits your baby could have.

Intensity—Highly intense babies have powerful responses. They will cry loudly. Less intense babies tend to be calmer and quieter.

Persistence—Very persistent babies take on challenges. They do not like to be stopped in the middle of something (e.g. stopped during a feeding to get a diaper changed). Less persistent babies can be persuaded to move on and come back to an activity. Persistent babies can accept only a little modification in their schedule. They are bothered by surprises or changes in plans.

Sensitivity—Highly sensitive babies have their feelings hurt easily. Have you ever observed someone make a face at your baby, and he started to cry? You may think he was crying without a reason, but the sight obviously bothered him. Less sensitive babies are not as concerned when others act in an unusual or surprising fashion.

Perceptiveness—Highly perceptive babies get distracted easily. Less perceptive infants notice less of what is going on around them.

Feeding Your Baby

It is very important that you are emotionally present during your baby's feedings. This is a routine time for your baby, and it lends itself to bonding experiences between you and him. You can explore the many feeding options that are available to you: you can breastfeed, use formula, or do a combination of the two. Each has its own advantages and disadvantages when it comes to nutrients, cost, and convenience, but what is sometimes overlooked is the bonding parents and primary caregivers have when feeding their babies.

Bonding While Bottle Feeding

Emotional bonding will also occur if you are a parent who has chosen to bottle feed. Bonding actually occurs in many of the same ways as with nursing. **The simplest thing you can do when you feed your baby is engage in skin-to-skin contact.** By taking off your shirt and feeling your baby's skin against yours, you are boosting levels of the love hormone oxytocin between you and your baby.

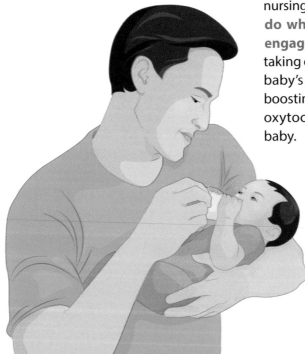

The most important thing to remember when bonding with your baby is to be present and in the moment while feeding him. Don't engage in distractions such as the TV, reading, or talking to another person. Make eye contact with your baby, and bring him close to you while you talk gently and smile at him.

3. Language Development

> **Language development is the effective way your baby combines cooing sounds, gurgling sounds, babbles, smiles, and cries to communicate different needs.**

Your baby is learning about language well before she will speak any words. Most babies have a natural head start from listening in utero; by the time your baby is born she will already show a response to her native language. Your baby even has the ability to use her sense of hearing to distinguish between nouns, verbs, and adjectives.

During the ages of three months to a year, a lot of language development is happening. You will hear her coo and laugh, play with sounds, and babble as she begins to communicate with gestures.

You are the most significant adult with whom your baby will interact and communicate. The way in which you respond to and engage your baby will support language development during these very important early years.

Cultivating Language

Receptive Language

Babbling

Nonverbal Language

WHOLE CHILD: INFANT
Language
Development Components

1. Receptive Language

Receptive language is the ability to understand or comprehend speech that is heard or read. Productive language is speech that is produced. Infants are better with receptive language than productive language because infants understand verbal communication better than they can produce it.

2. Nonverbal Language

Nonverbal communication includes facial expressions, the tone and pitch of the voice, and gestures displayed through body language. Nonverbal communication is especially important because your infant does not have the ability to communicate wants and needs through words.

3. Babbling

Babbling is when your baby appears to be experimenting with uttering articulate sounds but not producing any recognizable words. Learning to talk occurs in stages, beginning with sighs and coos, which are followed by strung-together consonant-vowel sounds.

4. Cultivating Language

Care for and encourage the growth of your infant's language development and explore specific ways you can prepare her for literacy development. Cultivating language involves your speaking to your child, reading to your child, and responding to her attempts to communicate with you. Engage your baby. That is how she will learn to engage with verbal and nonverbal language.

Even at the babbling stage, eye contact with your child helps him learn how to interact and to communicate with others effectively.

Receptive Language >
I Understand

Receptive language involves your baby's ability to listen and understand words.

ACTIVITY

One simple way your baby is developing his receptive language skills is by listening and making meaning during routines. For instance, Mom walks into her son Aiden's room and says, "Good morning, Aiden!" as she picks him up from the crib. Then she proceeds with the morning or afternoon routine.

INSIGHT

Aiden's listening to Mom, along with experiencing the action of being lifted up, leads to his understanding that it is time to wake up. The sequential activities that follow reinforce this understanding.

Before your baby was born he was learning language. Even while in utero your baby was listening to the sounds and speech of your voice.

Listening leads to your baby eventually developing literacy skills that begin right from the start. Receptive language is very hard to see in action, as much of it is cerebral. When your baby responds to the sound of a nice voice, he is displaying the beginnings of receptive language. This is also a sign that your baby is beginning to learn that communication is important and useful in his life.

If your baby is crying and hears your voice this will quiet him down as it is a familiar sound. This is your baby demonstrating that he hears you and understands you're a support person.

While your baby is still learning to understand oral language he may appear to be comprehending what is being said because he is picking up key words (e.g. "Good morning, Aiden!") and getting visual information from the environment or from gestures by parents (e.g. experiencing Mom pick him up). This enables your baby to learn language in a relatively predictable pattern (listening leads to understanding).

Receptive language is important for your baby's development because it will help him communicate successfully. For instance, have you ever wondered why doctors want a baby to cry when he is born? A good vocal cry is a sign that the lungs are developed and that your infant has a voice. Your baby uses his voice to communicate that he needs you to help him feel safe and loved. This is the only way your baby knows how to communicate to you at birth.

Support the development of your baby's receptive language skills by making eye contact as you speak to your baby. He will be better able to see your lips move as he listens to your words.

Remember: Listening leads to understanding, and understanding leads to your baby's ability to follow directions during his toddler years and develop meaningful social experiences with others in his environment.

Milestones in baby's receptive language development include:

* smiling when he hears your voice;

* looking for the source of new sounds at four to six months;

* responding to requests ("Give it to Mommy") at seven months;

* pointing to a few body parts when asked (nose, eyes, tummy) between 12 and 24 months.

Nonverbal Language >
Communicating Wants and Needs

Nonverbal language involves sending and receiving messages, both intentionally and unintentionally, in a variety of ways without the use of words.

ACTIVITY

Six-month-old Anna is in her highchair having baby biscuits. She starts playing with her food as if wiping the highchair clean with her hands. Dad notices, saying, "Anna, it looks like you are telling me you are all done. Let me take off your highchair tray, and I will get you out."

INSIGHT

Through Anna's gesture of playing with her food, she is using nonverbal language to send a message to Dad: "I am done."

Messages can be sent through a touch or a glance, eye contact, a gesture or facial expression, or a sound made by your baby. Since communication during the first year of your baby's life tends to be nonverbal, communication is said to be paralinguistic, or before words.

Your baby will express himself literally within seconds of birth by using his voice. As we discussed earlier, the voice, which was used when your infant was crying at birth, demonstrated his ability to communicate with you from that very moment.

By the first month, your baby is able to discriminate between all of the different sounds that people vocalize in every language in the world. She is able to learn just about any language out there, but her ability to produce sounds is extremely limited. This is the prime opportunity to start teaching your infant a second language; you will be amazed to see her use the language once she begins to speak.

The first type of nonverbal language your baby displays is usually reflexive, as when he cried. Other reflexive communication made by your infant includes movements and facial expressions. Non-crying vocalization is heard when your baby coos. At first, cooing will be done by accident, but as your baby develops, it will be done with intentionality. Cooing includes basic speech sounds such as "ooooh" and "eeeeh."

As you talk with your baby, you give her the opportunity to practice her coos and continue to make sounds from her primary language, the language you speak to her most of the time.

Nonverbal language is one of the key aspects of communication and is used by every person from the time they are young.

You will see your child use nonverbal language again when she repeats a verbal message (e.g. pointing in the direction of something) or when your child nods her head to mean "yes." Recall the famous proverb: "Actions speak louder than words." This is nonverbal language: action.

Sign Language

Sign language is a visual language that uses a method of facial expression (lips moving) and hand and body movements as a way to communicate.

Your baby can learn sign language at the same time she develops spoken language. When you give your baby access to sign language, you are enhancing the development of her linguistic, cognitive, social, and emotional abilities.

Sign language will give your baby a way to communicate several months earlier than babies who use only vocal communication. This will also help to ease frustration between the ages of nine to 12 months when babies are beginning to know what they want and need but lack the verbal skills to express themselves effectively.

As you teach your baby sign language, keep in mind the word **Ma.S.K.S.**

* **Ma**ke it interactive. Have your baby sit on your lap on the floor and hold her arms and hands to make the sign.
* **S**et practical expectations. Babies will not be able to communicate with sign language until eight months of age.
* **K**eep the signs simple and relatable for them, such as teaching *more*, *eat*, *daddy*, and *mommy*.
* **S**tay patient. Your baby will not do the signs correctly from the beginning; as she matures and with practice she will improve.

MOMMY

DADDY

GRANDMA

EAT

DRINK

GRANDPA

MORE

Remember, the Whole Child Parenting Program offers appropriate developmental products and monthly activity books that walk you through supporting your child's skills. Using these in conjunction with the recommended age-appropriate room materials ensures faster development.

Babbling >
Experimenting with Sound

As your baby hears vocalization by others, she is inspired to communicate back with her own vocalization patterns.

ACTIVITY

 Mom is staying home with her baby girl all day while her husband goes to work. One day, her husband comes home, and her seven-month-old daughter blurts out, "Dada!" Mom's heart sinks. She wonders how her baby says "Dada" first when she is the one caring for the baby every day.

Of course during this time, her husband is walking around the house like a proud peacock, texting everyone he knows; however, in reality, her daughter says "Dada" first because it was simply easier for her to say than "Mama."

INSIGHT

Babies will say words that are easier for them to form with their mouths because they are still learning to control their lips and mouth movements. In knowing this, Mom can now feel better about hearing the baby say "Dada" before "Mama." The most important thing about repetitive babbling is that your infant is practicing making deliberate and precise sounds.

Between three and six months, your baby will begin to babble. This is in response to sounds that you or other people make.

Think about a time you were so tired and you yawned in front of someone. That person then said, "Please don't yawn. You are making me yawn." Babbling is similarly contagious for your baby; she babbles, then you talk, then she wants to babble some more, and it keeps going until one of you gets tired.

Babbling will continue for several months. Around seven months, your baby will add repetitive babbling to her repertoire. In repetitive babbling, she will repeat the same speech sound over and over again; an example of this is "dadadada."

Repetitive babbling occurs because your infant is learning to control her lips and vocal cords and make them all work simultaneously. During the seven- to ten-month period, babies begin to show a preference for speech, can distinguish intonations in the voice, and know how to take turns in conversations—all despite the fact that they still cannot speak.

In other words, the babbling really sounds like communication with pitch, pointing, and pauses that make statements and ask questions. It is a fascinating time to listen and respond to your infant engaging in reciprocal communication experiences.

Between 10 to 12 months, your baby will use protowords; these are words that are not exactly like the original word but close. You will hear "baba" for bottle or "Dada" and "Mama" for Dad and Mom. The differences between protowords and repetitive babbling are that now your infant is using two syllables as opposed to a string of sounds. Protowords move your infant even closer to the development of speech.

First words will usually occur between 10 and 13 months of age, and they will be nouns like "ball" and "Mama." There is nothing quite as exciting as hearing baby's first words.

The start of language communication is an exciting time for you and your baby. It is so important to make sure you are talking daily with your baby and speaking through routines such as diaper changes and feeding times.

Cultivating Language >
Build, Keep, Nurture

The best way to build your baby's language is to speak with him continuously.

ACTIVITY

 Colby's dad is kneeling at the side of his crib ready to have some one-on-one time while he prepares for his child's afternoon nap. Dad begins to tell Colby a story his father told him when he was a little child. In a deep voice Dad says, "Once there was a furry rabbit" (Dad rubs Colby's blanket on his arm), "who lived with his father in the grass. His name was Snugglebug." (Dad tickles Colby's belly.) "And his mother's name was Rabbit . . ." Dad continues his story to the end, and then he asks Colby if he enjoyed the story as he gives him a kiss on his forehead.

INSIGHT

As Dad is talking to his son he is using shorter, simpler sentences, which he utters more slowly. Dad also provides an action to some of the words after he says them. This makes it easier for Colby to understand what Dad is saying. As Dad talks with Colby he is not only building his child's language skills, but he is also helping him develop his brain. Just like a baby needs food for physical growth, a baby also needs language for his brain development. The great thing is, language nutrition is free! You don't have to have fancy toys or expensive books. All you have to do is talk, interact, and engage with your baby in everyday conversations.

Speaking can include describing his feelings and expressing them out loud. Talk about the day and what he is eating. For instance, when you give him a bottle, you can say: "You are so hungry, and I have some warm milk for you. I will sing to you while you drink."

Tend to your infant's language development by paying attention to how you use language with him. One of the most common speaking techniques parents use with their infants is called "motherese."

In the above example with the bottle, Dad was using **motherese**, or baby talk. Motherese is "infant-directed talk," which is a non-standard form of English that is exaggerated and typically done in a high-pitched voice. Babies prefer motherese to adult-directed speech because motherese makes it easier for the baby to understand the structures of speech.

Motherese is important to use with your baby because it helps him learn to identify where words begin and end and gives clues needed to help in the development of his own language. Use correct grammar with your infant early on so as to not confuse him or teach bad habits.

Another simple method to develop your child's language skills is reading to your infant. In the beginning, your baby will not understand what is being read, but he will as time goes on; he will even want to participate. During infancy, reading enables you to look after your infant and have quality time with him.

Your baby has a desire for you to communicate with him, hear how he is doing, and babble together. Remember the yawning scenario: If you talk, your infant will talk back, and you can keep talking together.

Five simple ways to nurture your baby's language development:

1. Talk, talk, and talk. Your baby likes to hear a singsong speech, which means that the tone and pitch of the voice fluctuates a lot (as if you were singing) and is coupled with exaggerated facial expressions. Your infant prefers singsong speech because he likes the high-pitched sounds and watching your face when you talk to him. When your baby starts babbling, babble back with similar sounds. You will find that your baby babbles back to you.

2. Read, read, and read. It is never too early to read to your baby. It creates a perfect opportunity to bond with him. Your child will like listening to the sounds and rhythms of your voice. Pick stories that have lots of pictures and different textures; this will enable your baby to interact with you during the reading time.

3. Hold your baby's hand and let him touch the pictures. Name animals, colors, and other pictures in the book.

4. Follow your infant's lead. If your little one is giving more visual attention to a picture in a book, don't turn the page. Let him look at the picture as long as he wants.

5. Enjoy music together. Sing songs with your baby. He will love the rhythm and will be soothed by your voice. Songs like "Hush, Little Baby" will help your baby learn patterns and intonations of language. As your baby grows older, he will enjoy singing the songs with you. Music will lead to language learning as it allows your infant to watch your mouth, lips, and face as you form the words to the song.

Keep developing language with your infant by copying his sounds and encouraging him to imitate you. Put words to your child's sounds. Not only does your speech during this period help your baby learn to recognize speech sounds, but it is also how your infant will learn to take turns in a conversation and keep communication going as he grows.

4. Creative Development

> **Creative development reflects how your baby responds to colors, sounds, and movements. It occurs when he looks at different colors in books, interacts with puppets, or sways to music.**

From birth, your baby responds to contrast, colors, sounds, and movements. How your baby integrates these experiences will have an influence on her growth and development in many areas, not just creativity.

Creativity is developed through the various ways you interact with and respond to your baby. This can be seen in the ways that calm, soothe, comfort, engage, amuse, delight, and enthrall your baby. Playing creatively with your baby fosters many aspects of development. The physical skills creativity promotes become the primary way that your baby will learn about the world around her, thus giving her new ways of thinking, engaging, problem solving, and discovering.

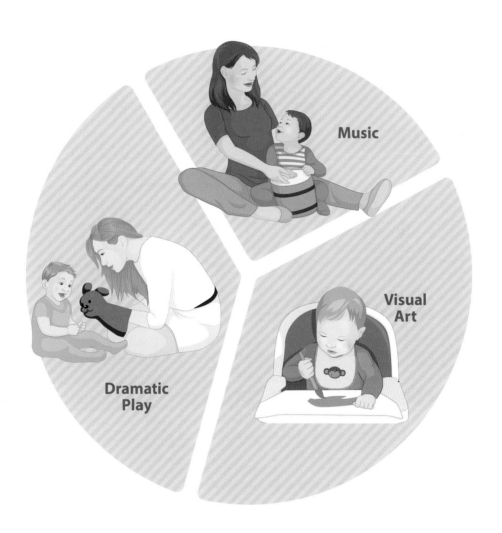

WHOLE CHILD: INFANT
Creative
Development Components

Creativity is a process and not a product for babies; they are still developing the coordination to control and manipulate objects with intention; they are also still developing the cognitive ability to problem solve and organize their thinking.

1. Music

Music is creative play with sound; it occurs when sound meets imagination. Any experience—from the shaking of a rattle to the babbling noises from your baby—that involves the basic attributes of sound is potentially musical for your baby.

2. Visual Arts

Visual art development occurs when your baby is able to experiment with a variety of colors and drawing instruments (like paint brushes) to develop color awareness. During visual art experiences he will experiment with the marks that can be made on different surfaces by his hands with paint as he explores the relationship between how things feel and how they look.

3. Dramatic Play

Dramatic play encourages the development of babies' social and emotional skills (sharing, taking turns, conversing, understanding, and managing feelings). Creativity, problem solving, and language skills are developed through dramatic play, allowing your infant to learn that there are things she can control.

From the very start, dramatic play helps build creative skills and stimulates the imagination.

Remember, the Whole Child Parenting Program offers appropriate developmental products and monthly activity books that walk you through supporting your child's skills. Using these in conjunction with the recommended age-appropriate room materials ensures faster development.

Music >
Instrumental and Vocal Sounds

Music is very powerful for your baby as it opens doors for her to become more balanced and healthy, both physically and emotionally.

Engaging in music play with your baby will help build the bond between you and she. Think about a time when you sang a soft lullaby to your baby, and she locked eyes with you, listening to your voice and watching your facial expressions. It almost seemed as if she was instantly mesmerized and soothed.

Musical experiences for your baby will promote learning in other areas of development. Think about where your baby is developmentally. Is she grasping objects such as rattles and small toys? When you give your baby a rattle to grasp with her hand, you are helping your baby develop her physical abilities (fine motor skills) and encouraging her to shake and make music with the rattle.

By taking the time to talk to her during the experience of holding the rattle ("I see you are holding the rattle with a firm grasp. That is a good shake you did!"), you then promote physical development with praise in her burgeoning musical abilities (making noise by shaking).

Next, support her musical creativity by grabbing another rattle or maraca for yourself and shaking it to a beat. **Your baby will attempt to imitate you, thereby further developing her musical creativity.**

ACTIVITY

 Once a week Nina and her mom attend a baby music class in the area. "Hello, everyone. We are going to play with drums today. Parents, place your baby in between your legs and the drum should go in front of your baby," says the teacher. She begins to hand a drum to Mom. Mom sets the drum in between Nina's legs and lets her bang on the drum any way she likes. She then gives it a try herself by tapping with a rhythm. Mom gives Nina praise and encouragement by saying, "You just made music, Nina! Hurray for Nina!"

INSIGHT

In this scenario, Mom is teaching rhythm to Nina. The wonderful thing is it does not look like Mom is teaching at all. As Mom is sitting on the floor with Nina tapping on the drum, she emphasizes the rhythms that a drum can make. Mom is amazed at the elation and joy that music brings to Nina. By bringing her baby to a group music class she is introducing the beginnings of music education.

"You just made music, Nina!"

Other activities you can do to develop your baby's musical skills include making it part of her bedtime routine. Play music while you give your baby a bath, or play a CD to help her relax and fall asleep independently. It does not always have to be classical music that you play; try some jazz or country. Sing to your baby, even if you think you can't do it so well!

Singing to your infant is the best way to expose her to music because she can watch your mouth movements and model your movements and facial expressions. You will see and hear your baby cooing and mimicking sounds heard in the song.

Avoid having your baby in the bouncy seat placed in front of the TV; instead, turn on your music player. Stereos are the next best thing to you singing and are much more beneficial for your baby's imagination and creativity than TV. Instead of watching characters dance or sing on the TV, your baby will use her imagination to begin to see how to move her body to music.

Take your baby to music in the park experiences in your neighborhood so she can see a live performance and hear how music is created. Also, invest in simple musical instruments such as rhythm sticks, shakers, jingle bells, a drum, and a xylophone. Let your baby explore the different sounds that each instrument makes. Have a concert with the two of you playing all the instruments you have. What fun!

Make sure to introduce songs and rhythmic chants that have actions your baby can watch or do with you, such as "Itsy Bitsy Spider" or "Pat-a-Cake." When parents expose their babies to music, they also support the development of good listening skills from an early age.

By making music a fundamental ingredient in your baby's everyday routine, you are not only solidifying the bond that you have with her, you are also encouraging your baby to experience the beauty and diversity of sounds from around the world.

ACTIVITY

 Danielle and Ben are sitting on the blanket with Mom. Mom reads the story and starts to sing, "Old MacDonald had a farm, E-I-E-O. And on his farm he had a cow, E-I-E-O. With a moo moo here, and a moo moo there, here a moo, there a moo, everywhere a moo moo!" As Mom is singing Danielle begins to get on her hands and knees and is moving her head side to side almost as if she is moving to the beat of her mother's singing.

INSIGHT

As Mom starts singing Danielle begins to recognize that Mom's singing voice sounds different from the voice she uses to read the story. Your baby will recognize the melody of a song long before she understands the words and will react to the sound and beat of the music as she listens.

Visual Arts >
Born Sensory Learners

Your baby loves to experiment with different fabrics, textures, and visual objects in books.

ACTIVITY

 Mom is home with Levi on a cold and rainy Tuesday. Mom wants to have some bonding time with Levi, but she is unsure what else she can do besides read a book to him.

Mom remembers that she and her husband have just put together a photo album with pictures from the most recent family get together. Mom picks up Levi from the floor and takes him to the family room, where she removes the album from the shelf.

Together they sit and look at family photos as Mom describes each person to Levi. "Look, Levi, here is Grandpa with the fish he caught!" Levi reaches his arms out trying to grab the fish in the picture.

INSIGHT

When Mom brings out the photo album she shares a wide variety of photos of people with her son. Levi reaches out to the picture of Grandpa holding a fish, body language that shows that Levi is most interested in that photograph.

The visual art system in infants develops rapidly over the first few weeks after birth. **As early as nine minutes after birth, your baby will prefer to look at pictures and photos with color.** When parents look at pictures, they can verbalize what they like about it or what they would prefer to see. The point is to engage the baby.

A perfect way to introduce visual art to your baby is by simply looking at photos of people, especially familiar people. Introducing your baby to art early on promotes neuronal connections in his brain. You can watch your baby respond to large, colorful paintings and pictures via a visual fixation or a smile.

Visual art gives your baby the ability to learn about the world around him through hands-on learning experiences as well.

By the time your baby is between eight and 12 months, he can hold a large writing tool (crayon or chalk) using a fist grasp and feeling it between his hands. Tape a large piece of white paper to the table and watch your baby make marks and lines on paper; it is important to give writing materials to your baby and support him in their use. Let him draw whatever he likes.

You give your baby a sense of emotional satisfaction when he can make art. This comes from making the decision to make one mark or two on the paper, from the control he has over the materials he is using, and from the autonomy he

has in the decision to pick up the tool.

Visual art experiences do not require fancy materials. Use basic materials such as crayons and washable baby markers. Visual art is an open-ended learning opportunity, and a recognizable picture is not necessary to have at the end of the experience. The goal of visual art for your baby is the process of discovery.

Visual art plays a role in all areas of your infant's development. Visual art for your infant will develop him as a whole child and promote learning and growth in the following ways:

* develops visual-spatial relationships like that of hand-eye coordination skills through making marks on paper,

* creates an opportunity for your infant to develop a nonverbal language to express his feelings,

* promotes self-awareness and individuality,

* heightens perceptual abilities,

* provides an important way for your infant to learn about his world!

Dramatic Play >
Pretending

Dramatic play is your baby engaging in pretend play as a way to explore his world.

It is hard to imagine how dramatic play coincides with your baby's development, but the foundations for dramatic play begin in infancy. Peek-a-boo games between you and your baby are an example of a dramatic play activity in which your baby enjoys the sudden appearance and disappearance of your face.

Dramatic play supports your baby in other areas of development:

Cognitive skills are developed as your baby comes to understand the environment through dramatic play opportunities.

Emotional development is supported as your baby uses pretend play to cope with fears and other emotions as he imitates you and your expression of feelings.

Social development is supported as your baby engages in pretend play with you. Babies imitate the social behaviors they see in their environment and then use these behaviors for future social interactions.

Motor skills are supported as your

ACTIVITY

 Tyler's aunt Olivia has made a sock puppet for Tyler. It is red, and she has glued big black buttons on it for eyes. Olivia decides that she will use her sock puppet to entertain her baby nephew by putting it on her hand and talking in a funny voice. Tyler absolutely loves it, letting out a belly laugh that can be heard by Mom in the kitchen.

INSIGHT

Olivia is showing Tyler a dramatic play experience. Even though Tyler cannot verbally join in, he participates in the pretend play by laughing and responding to his aunt. Olivia, using tools (the sock and her voice) to play act, helps her nephew better understand how he can communicate with his aunt.

baby walks to push the play grocery cart or stands to play with a spoon.

Language skills grow as you engage in parallel talk by giving your baby the words for what he is doing.

When you take a peek-a-boo game and enhance it with the use of your infant's familiar stuffed animals, making them disappear and reappear, this is a simple example of introducing dramatic play into your baby's environment. Adding animal sounds and changing the position where the animal disappears and reappears encourages visual tracing.

Parents can provide various play materials to support dramatic play:

From birth to three months, give your baby things to look at and listen to, such as hanging objects like lightweight scarves that are within view but not within reach. This will enable your infant to look, track, and identify objects in space.

When your baby is between two and six months, provide toys such as teethers and empty food cartons. You can allow your infant to follow his own interests with the toys or you can use them in responsive play with him.

During the three- to eight-month period, give small plastic wheeled toys, which will allow your baby to manipulate how the object moves.

Join in play with him by pretending to drive the wheeled toy to a destination.

For the 8- to 12-month stage, small rocking horses and push toys are also great; your baby will learn about cause and effect as well as learn how things function and are best used.

Your baby will prefer to play with objects that look like the real things you use. Most of all, he will participate in dramatic play with your support and engagement. As your baby matures in age, he will imitate you and practice your roles.

There are many things a parent can do to promote dramatic play with their baby that do not require purchasing fancy toys and materials. Do some of the following and watch how your infant responds as you build a stronger bond together.

* Using a pair of old keys, sit with your baby and pretend to start a car and make the "vroom, vroom" noise. Then watch and see how your infant responds. Look to see if he tries to make similar noises.

* Show your baby his reflection in the mirror. Place various hats on his head and watch his response, then place hats on your head. Is your baby laughing or smiling?

5. Physical Development

> **Physical development refers to how your baby develops head control, strengthens neck muscles, learns hand coordination skills, crawls, and later learns to walk.**

So much will happen during your baby's first year. Before you know it, your once tiny baby will be an independent person, able to move around and communicate.

Physical development occurs especially quickly during the first two years of your child's life. Your baby's birth weight generally doubles by six months and triples by his first birthday. You will see your baby grow between 10 and 12 inches in length (or height), and his body proportions will change during the first two years. When your baby was born, most of his body mass was in the head. As he gets older, the rest of his body catches up.

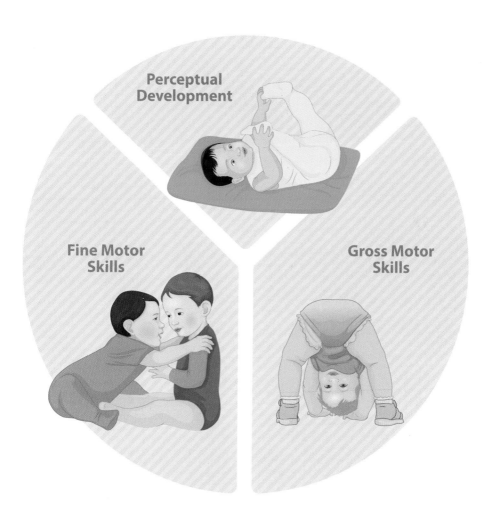

WHOLE CHILD: INFANT
Physical
Development Components

Infant motor development refers to changes in the capacity for voluntary physical movement. But before babies develop physical motor skills, they have simple reflexes. These reflexes facilitate babies' survival until they develop the ability to voluntarily control their own actions. This means that the first few weeks involve primarily reflexive movement; as growth occurs, your baby's reflexes turn into voluntary movements.

You will see some pretty important changes between birth and 12 months as your baby faces challenges that can only be solved by learning physical behaviors. It's all very exciting for a parent to observe baby's progress.

1. Perceptual Development

Perceptual development refers to the process of taking in, organizing, and interpreting sensory information. It is when multiple sensory inputs contribute to motor responses, i.e. when the senses tell the body what to do in response. For instance, when your baby turns his head in response to the visual and auditory cues he receives, he is exhibiting perceptual development.

2. Gross Motor Skills

Gross motor skills include the accomplishment of skills such as rolling over, sitting up, crawling, and walking. Gross motor skills enable your baby to move and gain different perspectives on his environment.

3. Fine Motor Skills

Fine motor skills involve the ability to hold writing tools (e.g. crayons), and participate in routines such as holding a bottle and eating. Touching, grasping, and manual manipulation give your baby experiences in learning about the features of people, objects, and the environment. Stacking rings and knob puzzles provide opportunities for your baby to practice fine motor skills.

The development of fine and gross motor skills happens rapidly in the early years, and it is important to provide your child with opportunities to build these skills.

Remember, the Whole Child Parenting Program offers appropriate developmental products and monthly activity books that walk you through supporting your child's skills. Using these in conjunction with the recommended age-appropriate room materials ensures faster development.

Perceptual Development >
Using the Senses

Perceptual development involves your baby learning to develop and use her five senses (touch, taste, hearing, smell, and sight) to explore the world around her through her developing motor skills.

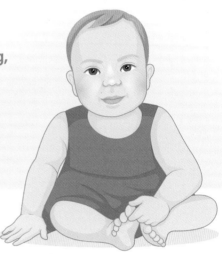

ACTIVITY

Mom takes Brooke to a baby gym class. Mom places Brooke on the floor in front of the infant climber. Brooke simply sits for a few moments looking straight ahead at the climber, then she begins to reach out her hand as if she is going to touch it.

INSIGHT

Brooke is using her perceptual information skills to make a choice about which motor action she will make (using eyes and hands to explore and observe equipment). Brooke is doing this before she decides if she even wants to crawl on the climber. Perceptual development combined with gross motor skills enable your baby to move and gain information and perspective on the environment she is in.

As a parent, it is easier for you to see gross motor skills than perceptual skills developing in your baby. For instance, you will see your baby start to raise her head during tummy time (gross motor skill), before you see how she is interpreting the world around her.

Think about when your baby turns her head toward you or reaches her arms out to you, you are not only seeing the gross motor skill, but you are also seeing how your baby uses her sense of touch and sight to connect with you. **In order for your infant to develop motor skills, she must see something in the environment that encourages her to act and then use her understanding to refine her movements so that she can interact with the world.**

Motor skills give your baby solutions to her goals of wanting to move and interact. For example, your baby will only learn to walk when the nervous system matures, allowing her to control certain leg muscles. This will occur when the legs have grown enough to support her weight and her desire to move. By working to develop your baby's perceptual motor skills, you enable her to move more effectively and with thought.

Typically, your baby will want to move when she is motivated by the challenge to cross the room; then she will initiate a few stumbling steps. Your baby will then refine those stumbling steps into smoother steps that are more effective for reaching the desired goal. Refining of steps happens through repeated trying and perception of the results obtained from that action.

It is important to note that even though the development chart in your physician's office may show motor development unfolding in a smooth, upward progression, this is not always the path your baby will take. Babies perceive things in their environment in different ways, and this will determine what motor path she takes. In fact, detours from the physician's chart will almost always occur as your baby develops at her own pace, and this is perfectly normal as long as she reaches the developmental milestone at the end within a few months of the suggested age.

ACTIVITY

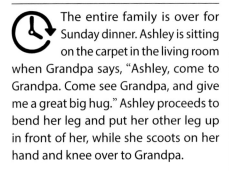

The entire family is over for Sunday dinner. Ashley is sitting on the carpet in the living room when Grandpa says, "Ashley, come to Grandpa. Come see Grandpa, and give me a great big hug." Ashley proceeds to bend her leg and put her other leg up in front of her, while she scoots on her hand and knee over to Grandpa.

INSIGHT

Ashley puts together the skill of moving in her own way to obtain the goal of getting a hug from Grandpa. It is most likely that in the doctor's office on the developmental chart, it does not say your baby will crawl by scooting on her bottom. As we know, this is not crawling, but it leads to crawling as your baby learns to get on all fours and move. On the other hand, some scooters skip crawling altogether and move right away to walking.

Think about your baby right now. Does she crawl with hands and knees on the floor? Does she scoot on her bottom with one leg extended? Or does she scoot with both legs bent at the same time? **No matter the way she moves, your baby is just thinking about how to reach her goal.**

There are many things you can do to support perceptual development in your baby as she uses her motor skills. Do at least one of the activities listed on the next page with your baby, and see how her skills develop.

Everything that involves your baby's ability to move goes into the category of motor development. When you work with your baby to improve perceptual motor skills, you help her move more successfully and with intention. One day soon she'll get where she's going all by herself!

Auditory perception:

The best thing you can do is read stories with your baby from birth. You do not have to read the words on the page, but you can focus on describing the pictures. Play different genres of music with your baby. Watch her reactions. Does she try to shake her body or move her head in response? Does she ignore it? Does she listen very carefully?

Visual perception:

To help your baby improve this important sense, engage her in activities that sharpen her understanding of what she sees. Lay her down on the floor and place some colorful patterned and checkered toys in front of her. Give her an opportunity to look for the toy by placing a few to the right or left of her eyesight.

Oral perception:

Let your baby taste new foods that are not too spicy or too sweet or too sour or too salty, but that feature one of these characteristics. Watch her pucker her mouth or suck furiously or chew excitedly or even spit it out.

Olfactory perception:

Let your baby smell different objects. It is possible that she may not understand to sniff in, but you can pass an object under her nose and away to see if she smells it and how she responds. Does she like the flower smell and try to grab it away from you? Does she linger or scrunch her nose at the smell of a cut lemon? This exercise can be challenging, but your baby is smelling different scents all the time in her environment.

Tactile perception:

Give your baby objects with different textures. Give her corrugated cardboard to feel or a fabric with raised patterns or a squishy, slimy toy and watch how she interacts with it. Does she repeatedly run her fingers over the edges or the surface? Does she recoil and move away? Does she poke at it? Does she try to put it in her mouth?

Gross Motor Skills >
Large Muscles

Gross motor skills involve the ability to control the large muscles of the body. These are associated with arms, legs, and torso.

Your baby's gross motor skills will develop before her fine motor skills, because gross motor development is from head to toe. **The first gross motor skill your baby develops is her ability to gain control of her head.** Control of the head is vital for your infant to direct her attention.

At birth, your infant's head was so heavy she did not have the neck muscles to lift her head; however, from around four weeks up to five months, you observed your baby develop her first large muscle skill (controlling her head).

Another major large muscle skill that develops in your infant is reaching. At birth, your baby reached without intention. She reached with no coordination between reaching and grasping, resulting in your infant reaching for objects but not accomplishing the goal of getting them.

Reaching develops in a timeline for your baby; between three and five months, you will see intentional reaching take place.

Between five and seven months, your baby uses guided reaching techniques. Her ability to coordinate her vision and control of her reaching has improved. As a result, she becomes more accurate and deliberate when reaching for an object.

By 11 months, you will see success; your baby can now use both hands equally for reaching and grasping. Even though you see both hands engaged in this process at this time, between nine and 13 months you will also see your infant having a preference for one hand over the other.

Now we have come to one of the best parts of gross motor development in your infant: WALKING!

On average, it takes babies about 12 months to learn how to walk because they have so many other behaviors to learn beforehand. As we discussed above, they must first learn how to reach. This is necessary in order for them to grab onto an object and pull themselves to a standing position or to maintain balance. Even before this, your baby has to learn to sit up without support, which occurs between six and eight months.

Practice will develop your child's gross motor skills. If she doesn't practice, she won't learn. So give yourself a break and put the little one down; let her learn to spread her wings and walk. Once a week do one of the activities below with your baby.

Runway for crawlers—Gather a towel and a small baby blanket. Lay them out in a line. Sit at one end and encourage your baby to crawl by cheering her on (you could say, "Come on, Tyler, crawl to Mommy. You can do it.").

Grab and go for walkers—Put one of your baby's favorite objects just out of reach on the front end of the couch. Encourage your baby to grab it and then bring it to you. This will encourage muscle coordination, motor planning, and problem-solving skills.

You must consistently support your baby's gross motor development through simple activities that are not based on the purchase of a product. **The development of your infant's gross motor abilities will be determined by the interaction she has with you.**

ACTIVITY

Marcus is sitting in his bouncy seat while Mom gets dinner together. Marcus is cooing and making all kinds of noises while sitting in the seat; in fact, he is so loud that it causes Mom to pause for a moment and just watch. On Marcus's seat he has a bar with several toys dangling down from it. As Mom watches her son, she begins see him thrust his hand forward almost as though he is throwing his hands at the toys on the bar.

Mom watches, trying to figure out what Marcus is doing. Sometimes he will reach the toy and other times he misses it. When he is able to reach the toy, he tries to open up his little fingers. This is when Mom realizes Marcus is trying to grasp the toys and he cannot do it just yet.

INSIGHT

Marcus is demonstrating what is called *ballistic reaching skills*; this is when your baby gets his hands into the vicinity of the object reached for, but corrections need to be made to have a smooth grasp of the object.

Marcus is still learning to gain control over his reaching and grasping skills. As he matures these skills will improve and thus support better hand-eye coordination.

Fine Motor Skills >
Small Muscles

Fine motor skills involve the ability to use the small muscles of the body, specifically the hands and fingers.

Fine motor skills begin to develop at the same time as gross motor skills; however, because your baby has to put her body in place first, the fine motor skills usually lag behind the development of gross motor skills.

As we discussed before with reaching, grasping occurs as your baby gets older. Initially, however, grasping will only occur when she accidentally comes in contact with the object or you place it directly in her hand.

The first big milestone in fine motor skills occurs when your baby is about nine months old. At this time, she is able to hold small objects between her thumb and forefinger, which is what is called the *pincer grasp*. This is extremely important because it paves the way for other fine motor skills such as writing and buttoning clothing.

Fine motor development involves skills that require your baby to control her eyes and head, as well as other muscles. Babies learn the art of controlling several different parts of their bodies through trial and error.

It begins as your baby learns how to control her eyes through focus and attention, and then she has to learn how to use her eyes with her arms and hands to create a fine motor movement. It is very complex and takes time.

Between 10 and 12 months, you will observe your infant being able to hold a spoon and feed herself, even though her aim will not be right on target.

Because fine motor skills are vital to the success of writing skills later in life, it is very important for you to support your baby's development. During everyday routines, encourage your baby to grasp objects by putting them directly in her hands or tapping the top part of the hand with the object.

You can stimulate your baby's sense of touch with simple materials like a scarf. Put your baby in your lap and show her the scarf.

Talk about the color and texture. Tell your baby that you are going to rub the scarf on her arms, legs, and face.

Watch for her to reach for the object as you touch each area. Depending on her age, you will see her just wave her arms, reach for the scarf, or actually grab it and close her hand. Activities such as these not only help build a bond between you and your baby, but they also develop her fine motor and tactile sensation skills.

As you are supporting and encouraging your baby's physical development, remember that everything works together. Gross motor skills develop with fine motor skills. Skill building happens over time and builds on past developments.

ACTIVITY

 Evan and his older brother are sitting together at the table. His brother is eating blueberry yogurt for an afternoon snack. Evan looks up at his brother with a big smile and then stretches his right arm out to reach and grab his brother's spoon.

Evan succeeds and is very proud that he is able to hold the spoon in his hand. Evan attempts to put the spoon in his mouth as he brings it up to his face. On his first attempt he only gets the side of his mouth. After trying a second time he gets some of his brother's yogurt in his mouth. Yummy!

INSIGHT

Evan is able to focus his attention on his brother's spoon and use his hand-eye coordination to grab it. Because he is still developing his fine motor skills he misses his mouth the first time, but after he tries again he succeeds.

6. Health and Care

> **Health and Care refers to the safety, grooming, self-help, and well-being of your child.**

Many parents do not understand some of the most common health procedures needed to care for their baby. The following pages cover health information that is easy to comprehend and can be applied to the routine care of your baby.

Mind
and Body

Hygiene

Sleep

Diet

Diaper
Changing

WHOLE CHILD: INFANT
Health and Care

Hygiene >
Bathing, Ears, Eyes, Nose, and Tooth Care

Bathing

Bathing is an excellent time for your baby to relax. **A couple of baths a week is generally all that is needed.** Bathing your baby every day will dry out his skin because it eliminates many natural oils.

Use a free-standing tub with a nonslip area for baby's back that is comfortable for your baby. Do not fill it with more than two or three inches of plain, warm water (not hot nor cold) and avoid soaps. Keep one hand on the baby and use a soft cloth to wash your baby with plain water and just a drop of mild baby wash.

Bath time for your baby is not only fun, but can also stimulate development. For instance, as your baby listens to you talk, he is also picking up speech patterns.

Ear Care

It may sound gross, but earwax is important in keeping the ear clean and healthy. Earwax is a substance that keeps dirt and foreign objects out of your infant's ear. **To clean your infant's ear, never use a cotton swab or insert anything into the ear canal. Your baby's middle ear is very short, and you could puncture the eardrum.** Use a damp washcloth to clean the outside of the ear if you see wax buildup.

Your baby's hearing

One to three months:
Your baby is born with fully developed hearing at birth.

Two months:
Your baby will begin to recognize and hear voices and respond to where the voice is coming from.

Three months:
Your baby will begin to coo and imitate high-pitched sounds and vowel sounds.

Four to six months:
Your baby will start to focus more on familiar voices and try to imitate sounds and words he hears. It is important to talk to your baby all the time and engage in two-way conversation when he babbles.

Seven to nine months:
Your baby begins to respond to familiar words and sounds, such as his name or the word "no."

His attention span is becoming more focused, and he begins to follow and search for familiar sounds and voices.

Ten to twelve months:
Your baby is beginning to make connections with the words and sounds he hears. He assigns simple words to objects such as ball, mama, etc. He points to familiar words or objects around him.

When engaging in sign language with your baby, mouth the word you are signing as well so he can imitate you.

Eye Care

Did you know your baby should have his first eye exam before he can walk? However, most children do not have an eye exam until they have reached the age of five. During your baby's first eye exam at preferably six months of age your pediatrician will simply check the basic working order (eye movement ability) and structure of his eyes to make sure everything is developing well. Your doctor will focus on your baby's eye movements and reaction to light or familiar objects. If your baby has clogged tear ducts, consult your pediatrician.

Cleaning

Your baby's eyes are very delicate and sensitive.

To clean your infant's eyes, use water and a soft cloth or cotton ball and wipe from the inside to the outside corners of the eyes. Make sure to wash your hands and use a different cotton ball or washcloth for each eye.

Taking photographs of your baby is so much fun. Have you ever wondered if the use of flash when taking photographs can cause harm to your baby's eyes?

No one can say for certain that a flash does or does not cause much harm; however, there are ways of taking a picture of your baby that do not require using the flash, and this is the safest way to get a picture of your little one. Take pictures in shady places and from directions that diffuse the light; you will get a better picture than one taken with one source of light (the flash) anyway.

Your baby's eyesight

One to three months:
Your baby can focus on objects 8–12 inches from his face and can track movement with his eyes.

You can help build your baby's eye muscles by locking eyes with him and moving from side to side as he follows your gaze.

He smiles as a response to seeing something familiar and begins to imitate gestures such as sticking out his tongue, licking his lips, spitting, and opening his mouth.

Two months:
Your baby can see color but not different tints and tones of colors. He focuses on primary colors and black and white.

Toys that are black and white with detailed designs or primary colors are best to buy for him at this age.

Four to six months:
Your baby can track objects as they move across the room. Infants begin to develop depth perception and understand that things exist even when they are not there. Peek-a-boo and toys that move in and out of view are great at this age. Your baby will start watching your mouth more and try to imitate the movements and sounds you make. His babbling will become more complex and include many "m" and "b" sounds.

Seven to nine months:
Your baby begins to respond to and imitate people's expressions and emotions.

Eight months:
Your baby's vision has developed to the point of being almost the same as an adult's, and he can see things farther away.

Nine months:
Your baby will recognize familiar people and objects, causing him to have heightened stranger anxiety when there are new people around or when he is in a new environment.

Ten to twelve months:
Babies can now judge distances fairly well and throw things with precision. Your baby will start testing depth perception through cause and effect by dropping things from the table or throwing them to see how far they will go.

Nose Care

With babies come a lot of mucus and drool. Mucus serves a number of purposes.

Mucus is a coating that both keeps germs from being ingested by your infant and acts as a thin layer of moisture that prevents tissues underneath from drying out.

However, it is important to keep track of your baby's comfort level and help her when she has too much mucus. When your child has a cold or allergies or there are drastic seasonal changes, your infant may produce more mucus as a response to the dry weather or to flush out more germs.

Avoid a nasal spray unless your doctor recommends one, and make sure the only nasal spray you use is a saline solution. Use a bulb syringe to help your baby "blow her nose" by sucking out excess mucus since she cannot do it herself.

Steaming in the bathroom as well as cool-air humidifiers are great ways to soften the mucus in your infant's nose before cleaning it. You can also raise the crib mattress so the baby's head is slightly elevated during sleep; however, never put a pillow or blanket under your infant's head when sleeping as it can cause suffocation; put an object under the mattress itself to elevate one end.

How to use bulb syringe with your baby

1. Squeeze the air out from the syringe and ensure that a vacuum is created.

2. Place your baby on the bed or changing table with her face toward you. Slightly tilt his chin.

3. Gently place the rubber tip of the bulb syringe in one of her nostrils and gently release the bulb to suction out the mucus.

4. Remove the syringe and make sure that the mucus is taken out in a tissue by squeezing the bulb with force.

5. Repeat the same process with the other nostril after cleaning the bulb syringe by wiping it.

6. Clean the inside of the bulb syringe using soapy water that can be filled in by squeezing and squeezed out.

Tooth Care

> **Average timeline of infant teeth developing:**
>
> **6–10 months:**
> lower bottom two teeth
>
> **8–12 months:**
> top two teeth
>
> **9–13 months:**
> top lateral incisors
>
> **10–16 months:**
> two lower lateral incisors

Your baby will get her first teeth between four and seven months old, though some children wait as late as 12 months or so to sprout their first tooth. The front bottom teeth are the first to appear, and the last teeth to appear are the molars.

All babies are different, and their teeth emerge at different times and affect them differently. Teething can be painful and can cause irritability and fussiness. You will notice her drooling more because her gums are very sensitive and swollen. Drooling can cause face rashes due to irritation from the constant moisture.

Discomfort in her mouth can cause your infant to refuse food and change her sleep patterns. Diarrhea or fevers (about 100.4° F) are not uncommon when your infant is teething. Talk to your doctor about teething gels or medication to help your baby with the pain. Chewing cloths, refrigerated teethers, or cold food (if your baby is old enough) can also help with the pain.

If your teething baby is uncomfortable during teething, keep things cool!

Chill your baby's spoon, teething ring, or sippy cup by putting it in the fridge for a few hours. The coolness will help reduce tenderness in the gums.

Diet >
Hungry?

Most babies initially lose between five and nine percent of their birth weight but will regain it by the time they are two weeks old. In the first month, your baby should gain five to 10 ounces a week and in months two and three continue to gain five to eight ounces a week.

Up until four to six months, your baby should be fed only formula or breast milk. Parents have the option of breastfeeding or using bottles with either breast milk or formula. Solid food should not be introduced yet because your baby's digestive tract is still developing.

Reflexes such as the rooting reflex and sucking reflex can help you as a parent to pick up on hunger cues and feed your baby in response.

The rooting reflex is your baby's search reflex for feeding. This reflex is triggered when you touch or stroke your newborn baby's cheek, specifically along the side of his mouth. Your baby will turn his head toward the side being touched, open his mouth, and seek something to suck.

The sucking reflex comes when a finger, pacifier, or bottle touches the roof of your baby's mouth. The sucking reflex will last for about three to four months after birth. It is an automatic response that helps your baby eat.

What your baby should be eating

0–3 weeks—Your baby should be drinking between one to three ounces every two to three hours, totaling about 8–12 feedings a day. An average baby should consume two to three ounces of formula or breast milk for every pound of body weight.

3 weeks–3 months—Your baby should be drinking three to four ounces and have between six and eight feedings a day.

3 months–6 months—Your baby should be drinking four to eight ounces and have between four and six feedings a day. At this time, your baby is sleeping through the night, so he will eat more in the morning and before bed.

Allergies

Allergies can cause vomiting, diarrhea, rashes, coughing, and or sneezing. Food allergies are one of the most common ailments that can occur during this age. Pets and insects can also cause an allergic reaction in your baby. After giving your child a new food, wait three days before giving it to her again so you can better monitor her reaction to it and see if she is allergic.

Your baby will most likely be allergic to the same things as you are, so be cautious when giving those foods and be sure to monitor her reaction.

Enough nourishment?

When breastfeeding, it is not always clear how much your baby has had to eat. Some signs that your baby is getting enough nourishment are:

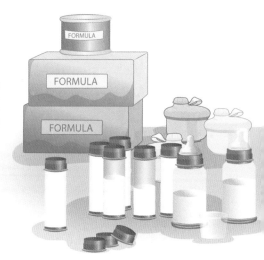

* Your breasts feel softer after nursing because they are less full of milk. After feeding, your baby seems relaxed and satisfied.

* Your baby has at least three bowel movements a day in the first month, and they are a yellowy mustard color.

Some signs that your baby is not getting enough nourishment are:

* Your baby is continuing to lose weight.
* Your baby does not reach his birth weight after five days of being born.
* After the first five days, your baby has small, dark stools.
* Your infant's urine is very dark and is the color of apple juice.
* Feedings take longer than an hour.
* Your baby is fussy and tired most of the time.

Formula makes it easier to measure how much your infant has eaten; however, it is important not to overfeed your infant. If your baby seems like he is still hungry, only give him only an ounce more to eat and do not assume that every cry or sucking reflex is an indication that he is hungry. A sign your baby may still be hungry is if he finishes the bottle quickly and starts looking around for more.

If your baby is overfed, vomiting may occur. Tummy pain or discomfort may also be a sign that your baby is overfed. **Infants show tummy pain by bringing their legs up to their tummies or tensing their bodies.** Check with your doctor if you feel your baby is overfed; your doctor can check your baby's weight.

Introducing Solid Foods

Between four and six months: you will start introducing solid foods.

At this age, you can start looking for cues that your infant is ready for solid foods. Most babies start solid foods around six months old. Solid foods at this age consist of semiliquid cereals or pureed foods such as squash, apples, carrots, and potatoes.

Begin gradually introducing solid food into your baby's diet. Start the first day with one teaspoon of pureed food or cereal that has been mixed with formula or breast milk. **If your child is resistant to solid foods, let him smell it or put a little on his lips and let him taste it and take a minute to think about it.**

Between six and nine months: your baby should be eating six to eight ounces about six times a day, totaling 32 ounces. Continue to give your baby formula or breast milk until he is a year old.

At this point, you can introduce a larger variety of solids such as pureed meats and other proteins. Increase solids at this point by ¼–½ cup total in two or three feedings.

Between nine and 12 months: your baby should be eating seven to eight ounces during each of three to five feedings a day, totaling 24 ounces. It is not uncommon for your baby to start drinking a little less formula or breast milk as more solids are introduced.

At this age, you can start introducing mashed foods and finger foods. Examples of finger foods include ripe bananas, peaches, and well-cooked pasta. It is also a good time to introduce O-shaped cereal, crackers, or small pieces of soft, cut-up bread to help with your child's teething. You should see your child start moving his jaw in a chewing motion at this age.

When your baby does not like something you offer him or is full, he will usually arch his back or turn his head away from you. If your infant does not like one of the solid foods he is offered, try again in a couple of days.

Bottle Storage

When feeding your baby using bottles, it is important to be safe and attentive. Because your baby is still working on holding up his own head, he will need a lot of support. **Your baby should be propped up at a 45-degree angle while feeding, and you should keep bottles out of cribs and especially away from changing tables.** Holding your baby while feeding is not only a great way to reduce the amount of air your baby swallows while eating, but is also a perfect opportunity for bonding.

Formula Storage

Store unopened containers of formula at room temperature and always check the formula's care instructions and expiration dates. Prepared bottles should be used immediately or refrigerated and given to your baby within 24 hours. Discard formula that your baby has not consumed within one hour. Do not use any harsh chemicals when washing bottles and nipples; soap and water are just fine.

Breast Milk Storage

Your breast milk changes as your baby develops, and it is important to use it as soon as possible after pumping it. The antioxidants in your breast milk are the most beneficial to your baby when the breast milk is fresh. It is also important to keep bottles clean and sterile.

When pumping breast milk, make sure to wash your hands and storage materials, as well as keep all storage materials in a dry, clean place. Because your breast milk is a bodily fluid, it is important that after you pump it you keep it between 60° F and 85° F (16° C–29° C), but only keep it for between six and eight hours. If you want to keep breast milk for 24 hours, you need to keep it fresh in a cooler with ice at 59° F (15° C) or freeze it. **When thawing breast milk, run warm water over the container until the milk becomes slightly warm. Separation is normal and can be alleviated by gently shaking the container.**

Do not use a microwave to heat the milk because it can create hot spots and burn your infant's mouth and throat. It is important that you do not refreeze thawed milk or feed your infant breast milk that has been thawed for more than 24 hours.

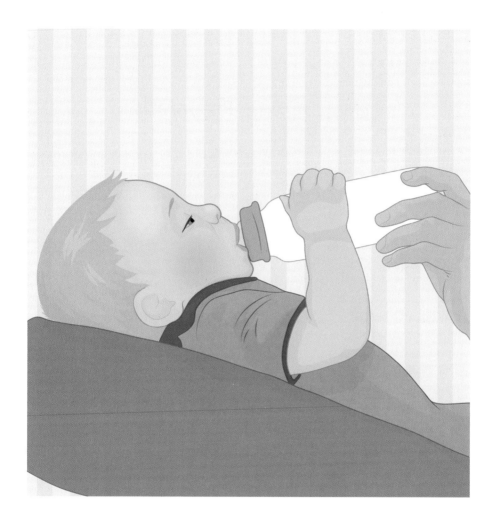

If you are worried about wasting breast milk, start with four ounces of breast milk in each bottle and heat up more if he is hungry so you won't have to throw away any unused breast milk.

Diaper Changing >

When it comes to diapering your baby, you can choose between disposable or cloth diapers. Also, while many parents purchase a changing table, there are other options such as changing mats or simply placing a towel down on a bed. **The most important thing to remember about your diapering area is that it should be easy to clean and have enough space for your baby to lie down safely.** Some changing tables come with a strap, but if you are changing your infant on a surface that does not, it is important to keep at least one hand on the baby at all times. Prepare your supplies before starting, and keep distractions to a minimum. Do not walk away from your baby at any time.

Preparation

* Make sure to wash and dry your hands before starting.
* Set up your diaper changing surface.
* Gather all of your supplies before you start:
  • clean diapers,
  • plenty of wipes or wet cloths,
  • diaper rash cream.

Diaper Changing Procedure

There are a variety of
ways parents can change
or prefer to change their
baby's diapers; however,
the following steps are
important when it comes
to the comfort, health,
and safety of your baby
when diaper changing.

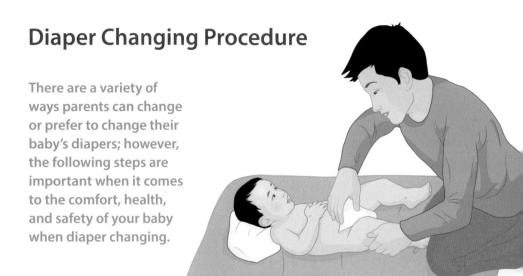

1. Place the new, clean diaper under your baby while he is still in his dirty diaper. Placing the clean diaper down first keeps the diapering surface clean and protects it from getting dirty.

2. Unfasten the tabs of your baby's diaper and remove it. If there is poop on the diaper, use the front half of the diaper to wipe the bulk of it off your baby's bottom wiping from front to back, especially for girls, because if stool gets into the urethra, it can cause a urinary tract infection.

3. Fold the top half of the diaper under your baby so the clean diaper does not get dirty while you wipe your infant's bottom. Dispose of the dirty diaper in a trash receptacle that is specifically for diapers and bodily fluids and has a lid.

4. Lift up his bottom slightly by gently grasping his ankles to properly clean him. Wipe his bottom with a wipe or damp cloth from front to back (toward his bottom).

5. If your baby has pooped, make sure to clean all of his creases by his legs and bottom so that he will not get an infection or diaper rash.

6. Add any creams if needed and place the front of the clean diaper on your infant and tightly secure it.

Wet diapers are one way to get an idea of whether your baby is getting enough milk to drink. Within five days after birth your baby should have three stools daily and five soaking wet diapers per day, though infants can go through up to ten diapers daily.

Change your baby's diaper frequently to avoid diaper rash or chafing that can occur from the moisture locked in the diaper. **Avoid using baby powder because your baby can easily inhale tiny particles of it that are light enough to be carried into the air and can cause respiratory problems.** If your child has sensitive skin, try switching to just water and towels because some wipes have alcohol in them that can dry out your infant's skin or fragrance that can irritate his skin.

Wash your hands and your baby's hands after you're done changing the diaper. Feces can cause illnesses or infections such as pink eye. Clean and sanitize the diaper changing area between uses with a bleach sanitizer solution, leaving the bleach sanitizer on the surface for at least two minutes (wipe or let air dry before use). Alternatively, you can cover the changing table with a larger cloth and just change the cloth after each use, cleaning the surface of the changing area with cleanser every

few days. Never give your baby a bottle or feed him on a diaper changing area.

Poop

Your baby is going through many changes, from his new surroundings to feedings, and his poop will reflect those changes.

One to two days old—Your infant's poop may consist of a dark blackish-greenish tarry substance that is a result of everything your baby ingested while in your uterus and that was left in his body after birth. Be gentle when cleaning this poop off your infant's body.

Two to four days old—Your infant's poop will be a mostly unscented, very dark shade of green almost black color because it is made up of ammonic fluid, skin cells, and other things ingested in utero.

After four days—Your infant's poop will start to lighten up and look greener.

Breastfed poop—will be a yellow, slightly green color with a thicker, mushier consistency, but it can be runny at times, especially in the beginning.

Formula fed poop—will be thicker like peanut butter and tend to stay more in the realm of tan, brown, or yellow coloring.

Solid food poop—will be thicker and a more distinct color of brown. Don't be alarmed if your infant's poop resembles colors of the food he ate or includes small pieces of food. This happens because your infant's food travels through his intestines quickly, and he may have swallowed some pieces before fully chewing them. Solid food poop also begins to smell more like adult poop.

Things to watch for:

* If your baby's poop is ever black (sign of digesting blood during breast feeding from a cracked nipple), contact your physician to make sure it is nothing more serious. Green,

yellow, or brown and runny poop can be a sign of an allergy or infection. Untreated, it may lead to dehydration.

* After you have started feeding foods, white poop could be a sign that your baby is not digesting food. All five colors (green, yellow or brown, red, and white) will require a call to your physician immediately. Also, as mentioned before, it is important to monitor your baby's poop when introducing new foods.

* Poop that has mucus in it can be due to your baby drooling; however, if you notice constant poops with mucus, it can be a sign of infection.

* Signs of constipation include poop that is hard and pebbly and often causes discomfort for your baby. Constipation can be due to introducing solid foods or even a lactose intolerance. Constipation can sometimes be accompanied by blood due to the hard poop irritating the anus on the way out.

* Diarrhea is very common and can come in the form of a "blow-out," which is usually very runny and made up of more water than solids. The color is very light and can occur in response to a new food. If your baby has been having diarrhea for more than a few days, contact your doctor.

Sleep >

Swaddling

Swaddling your infant is a great way to keep your infant comfortable and warm while sleeping. It is also a great way to keep your infant from being disturbed by the startle reflex.

To swaddle your baby:

Your baby should be snug but loose enough that his legs can move.

* First lay a blanket like a diamond on a flat surface and fold down the top corner about six inches, forming a straight edge.

* Then place your baby on his back so that the top of the fabric you folded over is at his shoulders.

* Bring your baby's arms down while you pull the left corner of the blanket over him.

* Pull the right corner of the blanket over your baby and tuck it in under his left arm.

* Then pull the bottom corner up, and finish by pulling the left corner of the blanket over your baby and tucking it gently under him. Some infants love the safety and security of being swaddled. Other infants may resist swaddling.

Sleeping Safety

There are a number of safety precautions to take when putting your little one to sleep. These precautions are especially important from birth to three months because of his inability to hold up his own head.

What to know:

* Your baby should be placed on his back to sleep, never on his stomach or side. When sleeping face down, your baby may overheat or rebreathe the air he just exhaled, causing a lack of oxygen.

* Avoid placing your baby on his side; he can accidently roll over on his tummy. **When your infant is about five or six months old, he will be able to roll over onto his tummy on his own.** If he is rolling over on his own, he may sleep on his tummy because your infant is demonstrating that he has enough arm strength to hold himself up and roll over again if needed.

* Do not have soft objects like toys, quilts, pillows, or crib liners in your infant's crib as they can cause suffocation. If your infant is chilly, dress him in warmer clothes when putting him to sleep instead of adding a blanket, but avoid overheating him.

* Never cover your baby's face with a hood, hat, or blanket and make sure there is fresh air and proper ventilation in the room. Swaddling can help your baby sleep soundly on his back, but it is important to make sure the blanket is tight enough not to unravel but not so tight that your infant will overheat.

* Sleep in the same room as your infant for about the first 12 weeks so that you can hear him wake up when he is hungry, wet, or uncomfortable. It is okay to sleep with your infant in the room, but do not have him share a bed or sleep with another infant or sibling. Alternatively, you can use a sound or video monitor; just make sure it is close enough and acute enough to pick up all sounds your infant may make.

Warning: Infants can make strange noises all night long. Some sound like dolphins, others make grunts, and sometimes a baby will wail in his sleep—and they can do all this and not even wake up.

* Don't give your infant a bottle in his crib because he is not elevated enough to drink it safely; however, pacifiers are great when putting your infant to sleep because the sucking motion soothes and calms him as he falls asleep.

Create a Safe Environment

During the 7- to 12-month period, your baby will explore everything in her environment.

* Take time to check and baby proof the corners of all furniture and cabinets.

* Attach barriers or gates to the top and bottom of stairwells.

* Cover all electrical outlets.

* Use fasteners to "lock" all cabinets below waist level.

* Pull electrical cords out of reach.

* Doorknob covers can be added to close off rooms to children once they become walkers.

How much sleep?

Between birth and about four weeks:

Babies need about 16–17 hours of sleep every day. They tend to sleep between one to two hours at a time, and these sleep times are scheduled around their eating times, which are every two to four hours.

Four to six weeks old:

Your baby needs between 14–16 hours of sleep.

After eight weeks:

Your baby will begin to sleep more through the night and less during the day, but he will still wake up during the night to eat.

Between three and six months:

Your baby will begin to establish his own sleep schedule and be fairly consistent with it.

Around four months:

Infants need about five naps a day.

At four months:

Changes will occur in the usual sleep schedule as he is adapting to a schedule that now includes sleeping longer at night.

At six months:

Your baby will be taking three to four naps a day. Your baby is consuming enough calories that he can sleep comfortably through the night for about five to six hours without needing to wake for a feeding.

Remember that each child is different. Some babies will sleep through the night at six months, others will take a year.

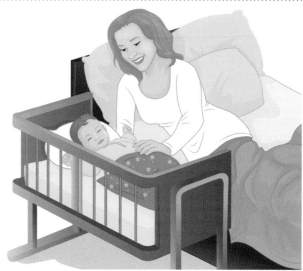

Sleep Training

Night weaning starts around six months as you start developing more of a routine for your infant with eating and sleeping schedules. As he wakes up in the night, try to soothe him back to sleep by patting his back or rocking him. **Do not force night weaning on your child. If he is crying for long periods of time, tend to him and attempt to night wean again in a couple of weeks.**

* At eight months old, your baby will begin to self-soothe back to sleep if he wakes up. Infants usually start moving toward a two-nap schedule at this age and will continue to follow that two-nap schedule until the infant reaches toddler age and switches to one nap.

* Remember that each child is differ-ent, and there are a number of different ways to sleep train or night wean your infant. The most important thing to remember is to make your child comfortable and happy.

* Your infant will let you know if he is not ready, and you shouldn't push him. If your infant is having a hard time keeping a consistent sleeping schedule, try another approach or try again in a couple of weeks. Stressing out yourself and your infant will not make it easier for either of you to sleep.

* **Sleep training is important, but so is building trust with your child.** If he has not calmed down after two or three minutes, tend to his needs and comfort him. Happy baby equals happy parent.

Mind and Body >
Yoga

Babies benefit greatly from participating in yoga.

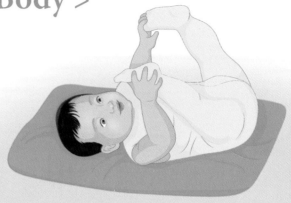

Yoga encompasses the whole body and is beneficial for both body and mind. It can set a foundation for your infant at birth for future exercise and movement while also promoting less stress and calm behavior, which can lead to better sleeping and a calmer temperament.

Through the movements of yoga (which you will have to simulate most likely as your child will not have the motor skills to accomplish the movements on his own), your baby's organs are being massaged and stimulated, specifically those organs in the digestive and nervous systems. Physically, you and your baby are exploring body movements more, which will make your baby more confident with his physical abilities and can build his self-esteem. Try lightly massaging his body, pushing his legs gently into his tummy and stretching them out gently, and pulling his arms out gently and gently pushing them in.

Stimulation of the nervous system can calm babies between feedings and before going to sleep, which helps with the balance of their daily routine. Stimulation of the nervous system can also contribute to brain and cognitive development.

Yoga is another great opportunity to bond with your baby as you lie together and explore his body through nonverbal communication. By having this opportunity for calm, nonverbal communication, you are building the groundwork for his future social interactions.

Get into doing yoga and massage with your child on a regular basis to start him off on the right path for regular exercise.

While your infant is too young to imitate and practice poses with you, he will nonetheless benefit from physical activity with you.

Remember, the Whole Child Parenting Program offers appropriate developmental products and monthly activity books that walk you through supporting your child's skills. Using these in conjunction with the recommended age-appropriate room materials ensures faster development.

Reaching Milestones >

You will see your baby's development by how he plays, learns, and speaks (babbles). As a parent you play a critical role in his development. Providing a safe and loving home and spending time together— playing, singing, showing picture books, and even just talking—will make a big difference!

Although babies develop through a generally predictable sequence of steps and milestones, they may not proceed through these steps in the same way or at the same time as their peers. Your baby's development is also greatly influenced by factors in his environment and the experiences you provide him. The information below is a guide to explain what an average baby might achieve. These skills may not occur at the exact times listed; skills can occur within a six-month to a year range. Consider what you read in the context of your child's unique development.

COGNITIVE

- **Birth–3 months:** I will repeat movements to master them, this will stimulate my brain cell development.

- **4–5 months:** I am curious about my environment as I watch what is going on.

- **6–8 months:** I will explore my environment through trial and error tasks (drop the toy and watch you pick it up for me).

- **8–12 months:** I am a baby scientist. I want to explore during every waking moment so I can figure out how everything works around me. How can I get you to read my favorite book? How can I get the block out of the box?

SOCIAL-EMOTIONAL

- **Birth:** I am learning to trust my parents and other caregivers in my environment.

- **3–4 months:** I will settle down when my parents comfort me.

- **5 months:** I can smile, and you can smile back at me. I smile and gurgle when I am happy and excited.

- **6–9 months:** I can tell the difference between people I do and do not know. Sometimes you may see that I am afraid of strangers.

- **9–10 months:** I love to play games like peek-a-boo with my mommy and daddy, even others who will play with me. When I want you to keep playing with me I will signal by waving my arms and legs and make sounds to let you know I want to keep playing.

LANGUAGE

- **Birth–5 months:** I have different cries, facial expressions, and body movements to tell you I am sleepy, hungry, wet, uncomfortable, overwhelmed, or I want to play.

- **3–6 months:** I begin to babble to you.

- **7–9 months:** I'll begin with vowel sounds "oh" and "ah" then I will produce a full repertoire of sounds (*ma -ma -ma*).

- **8–10 months:** I can create long babbling sentences. I may be able to say a few words or say "baba" for bottle. I might push the cracker that I don't want off my high chair and say "nuh."

- **10–12 months:** I will point to pictures in books in response to verbal cues you will give me.

CREATIVE

5–12 months:

- I can clap my hands and move my body (head, arms) to a happy-sounding song.

- I can shake a maraca or mimic the sounds that you make.

- I like finger paints and will squeeze paint through my fingers.

- I like to squeeze slick dough because the texture feels good on my hands.

- I will play a game of peek-a-boo as I explore dramatic play concepts with you.

PHYSICAL

- **Birth:** I have random uncoordinated reflexive movements throughout the day. I will look for something to suck on, maybe my thumb or a pacifier you gave me.

- **3–5 months:** I can visually tracks objects with my eyes. I can kick my mobile and make it move with my feet. I can also shake a rattle and make a sound.

- **5–6 months:** I can reach and grasp for objects. If I can't reach it, I will roll over to get the object.

- **7–9 months:** I can sit in my high chair. Put me on the floor and I can push my head and torso up.

- **9–12 months:** I can go from a sitting position and get to another place by crawling or scooting. I can pull to a standing position when I want to see something. Sometimes I may stoop to get something or to help me poop. My hand-eye coordination skills are really improving.

HEALTH AND CARE

- I need a bedtime routine so I will know nighttime is for sleeping, not playing. Pick a reasonable time, such as around 7:00 P.M., and choose three or four things you'd like to do every night, such as bathing, drinking, reading a story.

- To prepare for my bath routine, gather everything you'll need: tub, hooded baby towel, diaper cream, diaper, lotion, and cup to rinse my hair.

- Sit down with me to give me a bottle or food so I can develop healthy eating habits and social skills.

Environment >
Infant's Room

Your baby's early learning and developmental experiences begin at birth and will continue through kindergarten.

Birth through age five is a distinct period of life for your child; the experiences she is exposed to now will set the foundation for her success in school and in other areas.

Environments that are stimulating for your baby are filled with safe objects to explore, allow freedom of movement, and provide a variety of experiences.

The most important aspect of a stimulating environment is how you create an inviting, challenging play space in which your baby can interact with you.

The key to achieving this goal is to organize all materials using your **Six Drawer Whole Child Color-Coded Organizer**; this will enable you to access materials easily. It will help you focus because you'll choose which of the **six categories of development— cognitive, social-emotional, language, creative, physical, and health**—you and your baby will interact in.

The following picture shows what the recommended infant room looks like. The objects and materials shown will support you in creating a stimulating environment for your baby, one that is filled with specific furniture and age-appropriate toys to give her opportunities to practice all her new skills.

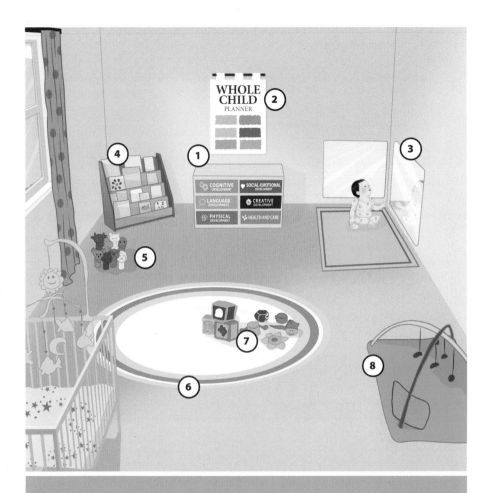

Whole Child: Infant's Room

The following list contains must-have items for your baby's room. These items will be used interchangeably with your other Whole Child Parenting materials.

1. Six Drawer Whole Child Color-Coded Organizer
2. Whole Child Wall Planner
3. Mirror
4. Bookshelf
5. Puppet/Pretend Play Materials
6. Carpet
7. Blocks and Soft Toys
8. Play Mat

1. Six Drawer Whole Child Color-Coded Organizer

Easily organize educational materials and toys by six areas of development. Ensure your child always has enough materials in each drawer.

2. Whole Child Wall Planner

Plan and organize weekly activities based on six areas of development.

3. Mirror

Helps develop self-awareness skills, a major step in social-emotional development.

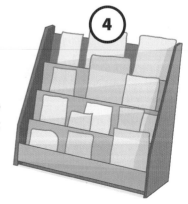

4. Bookshelf

Makes books easily accessible to child and supports independent exploration and literacy skills. Use for bonding with child through one-on-one time.

5. Puppet/Pretend Play Materials

Helps social communication, and interactive skills through shared experiences. Use for pretend play and peek-a-boo games.

6. Carpet

Provides a soft, safe place, free from clutter, for your child to play on. Use for providing materials in one central location at child's eye level. Enables parent to change out materials and still maintain child safety.

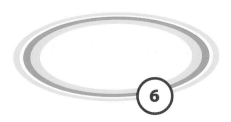

7. Blocks and Soft Toys

Helps child learn cause and effect, grasping, and reaching, and develops visual perception. Stacking, talking about colors, and exploration of textures develop hand-eye coordination skills.

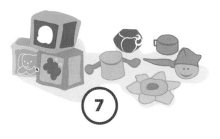

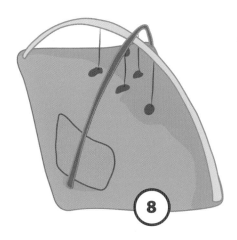

8. Play Mat

Provides a specific place to develop large and small muscle skills. Helps rolling over, reaching up, grasping, tummy time, visual skills, crawling, prevention of flat spots, and playing on left and right sides of body.

whole child activity books >

Have a look at a sample of
our series of activity books for
infants. This series of 4 titles
helps infants exercise their
brains and bodies in every
category of development
explored in the Whole Child
Parenting books. The 4 titles
are available now.

WHOLE CHILD

Activity Book

Transportation

WHOLE CHILD = $\dfrac{\text{smart} + \text{creative}}{\text{healthy} + \text{happy}}$

Infant
(Birth to 12 Months)

COGNITIVE
DEVELOPMENT

Problem-solving · Attention · Numbers

SOCIAL-EMOTIONAL
DEVELOPMENT

Self-control · Friendship · Feelings

LANGUAGE
DEVELOPMENT

Communication · Speaking · Literacy

CREATIVE
DEVELOPMENT

Dramatic Play · Dance · Music · Arts

PHYSICAL
DEVELOPMENT

Motor Skills: Sensory, Gross, Fine

HEALTH AND CARE

Hygiene · Diet · Routine · Yoga

sneak peek >

whole child parenting program >

Get a sneak peek into the
next book in the series.
Whole Child Parenting: Toddler
is a comprehensive look
into the development of
children ages 12–24 months.
The book is available now.

WHOLE CHILD
PARENTING

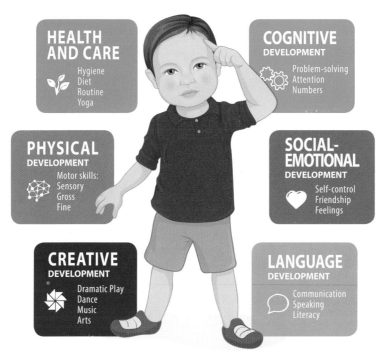

HEALTH AND CARE
Hygiene
Diet
Routine
Yoga

COGNITIVE DEVELOPMENT
Problem-solving
Attention
Numbers

PHYSICAL DEVELOPMENT
Motor skills:
Sensory
Gross
Fine

SOCIAL-EMOTIONAL DEVELOPMENT
Self-control
Friendship
Feelings

CREATIVE DEVELOPMENT
Dramatic Play
Dance
Music
Arts

LANGUAGE DEVELOPMENT
Communication
Speaking
Literacy

TODDLER
(12 to 24 Months)

Parents, educators, and caregivers
will learn how best to encourage growth and
skill-building in all six developmental areas.

sneak peek >

Milestones for a Toddler

 COGNITIVE — 1

- Begins to sort shapes and colors
- Matches pictures with objects
- Recognizes quantities of one to three

 SOCIAL-EMOTIONAL — 2

- Shows defiant behavior
- Shows separation anxiety
- Recognizes themselves in mirror

LANGUAGE — 3

- Says between 10 to 20 words
- Uses two-word sentences
- Follows one-step instructions

 CREATIVE — 4

- Can sing
- Explores art materials
- Dances to music

 PHYSICAL — 5

- Runs with ease
- Rides a tricycle
- Holds markers and crayons

 HEALTH AND CARE — 6

- Walks alone
- Uses cup and spoon
- Changes from two naps to one

toddler

Between the ages of 12 to 24 months your child is embarking on some new milestones and going through very visible changes. You will see your toddler's arms and legs are becoming stronger, which makes it easier for him to pull himself up to stand and move around. He is able to reach and explore more of his environment. However, with emotions at a high, this can cause some challenging behaviors and tantrums when he does not get what he wants. In this year we will help you with some tips to work with your child and their often challenging (but interesting!) behavior.

Whole Child Parenting: Toddler
Available now >

WHOLE CHILD

Parenting Program books and materials
are available worldwide.

Also available separately

Birth to Age Five

Parents, educators, and caregivers
will learn how best to encourage growth and
skill-building in all six developmental areas.

The book that kick started the program!

INFANT
(Birth to 12 Months)

Parents, educators, and caregivers
will learn how best to encourage growth and
skill-building in all six developmental areas.

TODDLER
(12 to 24 Months)

Parents, educators, and caregivers
will learn how best to encourage growth and
skill-building in all six developmental areas.

AGE TWO

Parents, educators, and caregivers
will learn how best to encourage growth and
skill-building in all six developmental areas.

AGE THREE

Parents, educators, and caregivers
will learn how best to encourage growth and
skill-building in all six developmental areas.

AGE FOUR

Parents, educators, and caregivers
will learn how best to encourage growth and
skill-building in all six developmental areas.

Whole Child Program Activity Books

- 4 **Infant** Titles
- 6 **Toddler** Titles
- 12 **Age Two** Titles
- 12 **Age Three** Titles
- 12 **Age Four** Titles

Whole Child Program books and materials are available at
special discounts when purchased in bulk for premiums and
sales promotions as well as for fundraising or educational use.
For details, please contact us at: sales@wholechild.co

Visit us on the web at: www.wholechild.co